MASTER LFCS 2024: UNLEASH YOUR POTENTIAL

Six Comprehensive Practice Exams with Detailed Answers for the Linux Foundation Certified System Administrator Exam

Ghada Atef

To all the aspiring Linux administrators, who dare to dream, strive to learn, and have the courage to unleash their potential. This book is a testament to your journey, a guide on your path, and a companion in your pursuit of mastery. May the knowledge you gain here light your way forward.

In the information age, build a ladder of knowledge, not a shelter.

ANONYMOUS

CONTENTS

PREFACE

In the ever-evolving world of technology, Linux has stood the test of time, proving itself as a robust and reliable operating system. The Linux Foundation Certified System Administrator (LFCS) certification is a testament to one's proficiency in this field, and this book, "Master LFCS 2024: Unleash Your Potential," is designed to be your companion on this journey.

This book is not just about passing the LFCS exam; it's about truly understanding the depth and breadth of Linux administration. It's about unleashing your potential. The six comprehensive practice exams included in this book, complete with detailed answers, are designed to challenge you, to push you to your limits, and to prepare you for what lies ahead.

Whether you're a seasoned professional looking to validate your skills, or a beginner stepping into the world of Linux, this book is for you. It's for anyone who believes in the power of knowledge, the importance of lifelong learning, and the value of certification.

As you delve into these pages, remember that the journey of a thousand miles begins with a single step. Each chapter you read, each practice exam you take, is a step towards your goal. Embrace the challenge, enjoy the process, and may the knowledge you gain here serve you well in your career and beyond.

Welcome to "Master LFCS 2024: Unleash Your Potential." Your journey begins now.

PROLOGUE

In the vast expanse of the digital universe, there exists a world that is both complex and beautiful, challenging and rewarding. This world is Linux, an open-source operating system that powers servers, systems, and networks around the globe.

The Linux Foundation Certified System Administrator (LFCS) certification is a gateway to this world. It is a badge of honor, a mark of competence, and a symbol of respect among peers. But the journey to earning this certification is not easy. It requires dedication, perseverance, and a thirst for knowledge.

"Master LFCS 2024: Unleash Your Potential" is more than just a book. It is a roadmap to success, a toolkit for problem-solving, and a source of inspiration. It is a beacon of light for those navigating the intricate pathways of Linux administration.

The six comprehensive practice exams contained within these pages are not merely tests, but stepping stones towards mastery. Each question is a puzzle waiting to be solved, each answer a lesson to be learned.

As you embark on this journey, remember that every great achievement begins with a decision to try. The path may be steep, the journey may be long, but the view from the top is worth it.

Welcome to the world of Linux. Welcome to "Master LFCS 2024: Unleash Your Potential." Let the adventure begin.

CONTACT ME

Thank you for grabbing a copy of my book **Master LFCS 2024: Unleash Your Potential!** I hope you found the book informative and helpful on your journey.

If you have any questions, comments, or suggestions, please feel free to contact me through the following channels:

Email: [linux.expert.eg@gmail.com]

Social Media:

[https://www.linkedin.com/in/ghada-atef/]

I strive to respond to all inquiries within 48 hours.

I am always looking for ways to improve my work, so your feedback is greatly appreciated. Thank you for helping me make this book the best it can be!

LFCS PRACTICE EXAM ONE

Question 1: Text manipulation

Assume, you have a text file named ~/myfile.txt containing the following:

- 100 lines.
- The word "Today".
- Some lines end with a period (".")

Perform the following operations on the file:

- Reposition Line: Move the fifth line to the beginning of the file, making it the new first line.
- Delete Line: Remove the forty-first line from the file.
- Replace Text: Replace all occurrences (case-sensitive) of the word "Today" with "Tomorrow" throughout the file.
- Append Newline: Add a newline character at the end of any line that terminates with a period (".")

Explanation

1. Reposition Line (head + sed):

# Use head to extract the first 4 lines and sed to insert the 5th line at the beginning
$ head -n 4 ~/myfile.txt | sed '5d; 1i\cat ~/myfile.txt | tail -n 1' > temp.txt

# Move the modified content back to the original file
$ mv temp.txt ~/myfile.txt

Explanation:

> *head -n 4 ~/myfile.txt:* This extracts the first four lines of the

file using head.

> *5d:* This deletes the fifth line using sed.

> *1i\cat ~/myfile.txt | tail -n 1':* This inserts the output of > cat ~/myfile.txt | tail -n 1 (which is the fifth line) at the beginning (line 1) using sed's i command.

> The entire command is piped to > to redirect the output to a temporary file (temp.txt).

> Finally, mv temp.txt ~/myfile.txt moves the modified content back to the original file.

2. Delete Line (sed):
```
$ sed '41d' ~/myfile.txt > temp.txt
$ mv temp.txt ~/myfile.txt
```

Explanation:

> *sed '41d' ~/myfile.txt:* This uses sed with the d flag to delete the 41st line.

> The output is redirected to temp.txt and then moved back to the original file using mv.

3. Replace Text (sed):
```
$ sed 's/Today/Tomorrow/g' ~/myfile.txt > temp.txt
$ mv temp.txt ~/myfile.txt
```

Explanation:

> *sed 's/Today/Tomorrow/g' ~/myfile.txt:* This uses sed with the s flag for substitution.

> *s/Today/Tomorrow/:* This defines the search pattern (Today) and the replacement string (Tomorrow).

> *g:* This flag replaces all occurrences (not just the first) on each line.

> The modified content is again written to a temporary file and moved back.

4. Append Newline (sed):

```
$ sed -e 's/\.$/\.\n/' ~/myfile.txt > temp.txt
$ mv temp.txt ~/myfile.txt
```

Explanation:

> *sed -e 's/\.$/\.\n/' ~/myfile.txt:* This uses sed with the -e flag to specify multiple editing commands.
> *s/\.$/\.\n/:* This replaces a single period followed by the end of line ($) with a period, a newline character (\n), using the substitution command (s).
> The modified content is written to the temporary file and moved back.

Important Notes:

These commands use temporary files (temp.txt) to avoid modifying the original file until the changes are verified.

Question 2: File Editing
and Text Processing

Assuming the necessary permissions are granted, complete the following tasks:

Within the /etc/configuration.cfg file, append a new line at the end with the content: serviceX=active. Save the changes and exit the editor. Confirm that the line has been added correctly.

Display only the lines containing the word 'active' in this file. Redirect this filtered output to /opt/active_services.txt. Ensure the existence of the /opt/active_services.txt file before redirection. If it doesn't exist, create it. Confirm the redirection of the output.

Automate a search and replace action on the /etc/configuration.cfg file. Replace all occurrences of the word enabled with disabled. Verify the correctness of the changes.

Explanation
1. Appending a new line
```
$ echo "serviceX=active" | sudo tee -a /etc/configuration.cfg
```

```
# Verification of the addition
$ tail -n 1 /etc/configuration.cfg
```

2. Displaying active services and redirecting the output
```
$ grep "active" /etc/configuration.cfg | sudo tee /opt/
active_services.txt > /dev/null
```

```
# Verification of the redirection
$ cat /opt/active_services.txt
```

3. Replacing 'enabled' with 'disabled'
```
$ sudo sed -i 's/enabled/disabled/g' /etc/configuration.cfg
```

```
# Verification of the replacement
$ grep "disabled" /etc/configuration.cfg
```

Explanation:

The echo "serviceX=active" | sudo tee -a /etc/configuration.cfg command is employed to append a new line to the end of the file. Here, tee -a is utilized to append the output of the echo command to the file.

To verify the successful addition, tail -n 1 /etc/configuration.cfg is used, displaying the last line of the file.

Next, to display lines containing the word 'active' and redirect the output to /opt/active_services.txt, we use grep "active" /etc/configuration.cfg | sudo tee /opt/active_services.txt > /dev/null. The > /dev/null part ensures that the output is not displayed on the console during redirection.

The correctness of the redirection is confirmed by cat /opt/active_services.txt.

Lastly, to automate the search and replace action, sudo sed -i 's/enabled/disabled/g' /etc/configuration.cfg is utilized, replacing all instances of 'enabled' with 'disabled'. The -i option ensures the changes are made in-place.

Verification of the replacement is performed using grep "disabled" /etc/configuration.cfg.

Question 3: User Management and Privileges

Create a new user account for John, and configure his system access with the following requirements:

1. Set John's login shell to /bin/zsh.
2. Set an initial password for John (example123).
3. Grant John administrative privileges by adding him to the admin group (secondary group).
4. Verify John's successful login and ability to use sudo.

Explanation

1. Create a User Account:
$ sudo useradd -m -s /bin/zsh john

sudo: Required for administrative tasks.
useradd: Command to create a new user.
-m: Creates a home directory for John.
-s /bin/zsh: Sets John's login shell to zsh.
john: Username for the new account.

2. Set Initial Password:
$ sudo passwd john

sudo: Required for administrative tasks.
passwd: Command to set/change user passwords.
john: Username for whom the password is being set.
(During prompt): Enter example123 as the new password twice.

Add User to admin Group:
$ sudo usermod -aG admin john

sudo: Required for administrative tasks.
usermod: Command to modify user account details.
-aG admin: Appends John to the admin group (secondary group).
john: Username to be added to the group.

Verification:

- Switch to the John account using su - john or ask John to log in with his credentials.
- Verify the login shell by running *echo $SHELL*. It should display /bin/zsh.
- Test sudo functionality by running sudo whoami. If successful, it should display root.

Question 4: File Searching and Manipulation

Complete the following tasks within the /opt/database/ directory, which contains multiple files with text content:

1. Search all files within /opt/database/ for occurrences of the word admin.
2. Once found, copy any file containing the admin string to the /opt/found/ directory. Ensure the existence of the /opt/found/ directory before copying. If it doesn't exist, create it.
3. Confirm the successful copy of the file(s).

Explanation

1. Searching for occurrences of 'admin'
```
$ grep -rl 'admin' /opt/database/
```

2. Copying the file(s)
```
# Ensure the existence of /opt/found/ directory
$ mkdir -p /opt/found/
```

```
# Copy the file(s)
$ grep -rl 'admin' /opt/database/ | xargs -I '{}' cp '{}' /opt/found/
```

3. Verification of the copy
```
$ ls /opt/found/
```

Explanation:

- The grep -rl 'admin' /opt/database/ command is employed to search for the word 'admin' in all files within the /opt/database/ directory. The -r option instructs grep to read all files under each directory recursively, while the -l option ensures that only file names of matching files are displayed.

- To guarantee the existence of the /opt/found/ directory, we utilize mkdir -p /opt/found/, with the -p option ensuring that parent directories are created as necessary.

- To copy the file(s) containing the 'admin' string, we use grep -rl 'admin' /opt/database/ | xargs -I '{}' cp '{}' /opt/found/. Here, xargs is employed to construct and execute command lines from standard input.

- Lastly, we verify the successful copy of the file(s) using ls /opt/found/.

Question 5: Bash Scripting

You have a bash script named ~/scripts/myscript.sh. Modify the script to achieve the following functionalities:

1. Direct Execution: Allow the script to execute directly by calling ~/scripts/myscript.sh from any directory.
2. User Identification: Print the username of the user who ran the script as the first line of the script's output.
2. Default Gateway Detection: Retrieve and display the IP address of the default gateway on the second line of the script's output.

Explanation

1. Direct Execution (shebang):

Edit the script (nano ~/scripts/myscript.sh) and add the following line as the first line:

`#!/bin/bash`
This line, called a shebang, specifies the interpreter (bash) to be used for running the script.

2. User Identification (whoami):

Add the following line to the script to print the username:

`echo "User: $(whoami)"`
whoami: This command retrieves the username of the current user.

echo: This prints the output of whoami with a descriptive label ("User: ").

3. Default Gateway Detection (ip route):

Add the following line to the script to extract the default gateway:

```
gateway_ip=$(ip route | grep 'default via' | awk '{print $3}')
echo "Default Gateway: $gateway_ip"
```

> *ip route:* This command displays the routing table.
> *grep 'default via':* This filters the output of ip route to lines containing "default via", which indicates the default gateway.
> *awk '{print $3}':* This extracts the third column from the filtered line using awk. This column typically contains the IP address of the default gateway.
> The extracted IP is stored in the variable gateway_ip.
> The final echo statement prints the label ("Default Gateway:") followed by the retrieved IP address.

Complete Script:

```
#!/bin/bash

echo "User: $(whoami)"

gateway_ip=$(ip route | grep 'default via' | awk '{print $3}')
echo "Default Gateway: $gateway_ip"
```

Explanation:

This enhanced script combines the shebang line for direct execution with commands to identify the user and retrieve the default gateway. The script utilizes common bash commands (whoami, ip route, grep, awk) and variable assignment to achieve the desired functionalities.

Important Notes:

- Remember to save the script after making the modifications.
- Make the script executable using chmod +x ~/scripts/ myscript.sh.
- This solution assumes a standard network configuration where the default gateway information is displayed in the output of ip route.

Question 6: Package Management

Install the tmux package.

Explanation

Both Ubuntu 20.04 and CentOS Stream 8 utilize package managers for software installation. Here's how to install tmux using the appropriate package manager for each system:

On Ubuntu 20.04:

Use the apt package manager:
```
$ sudo apt update
$ sudo apt install tmux
```

Explanation:

sudo: This grants temporary administrative privileges to execute the following command.
apt update: This updates the package list to ensure you have access to the latest versions.
sudo apt install tmux: This installs the tmux package using apt.

On CentOS Stream 8:

Use the dnf package manager:
```
$ sudo dnf update
$ sudo dnf install tmux
```

Explanation:

- Similar to the Ubuntu steps, this uses *sudo* for elevated

privileges and dnf for package management.
- *sudo dnf update:* This updates the package list for CentOS Stream 8.
- *sudo dnf install tmux:* This installs the tmux package.

Important Notes:

It's recommended to update the package list before installation to ensure you get the latest versions.

Question 7: Cron Job Management

Create a cron job that runs a script named "/scan_filesystem" owned by the root user every minute.

Explanation

1. Open the crontab file for the root user:
$ sudo crontab -e
This command opens the crontab file for the root user. Using sudo ensures that the command is executed with superuser privileges. Editing the crontab file allows us to schedule periodic tasks.

Add the cron job to the crontab file:

a. Option 1:
* * * * * pkill -f /scan_filesystem

b. Option 2:
* * * * * pkill -u root -f /scan_filesystem

c. Option 3:
* * * * * pkill -u root -SIGKILL -f /scan_filesystem

Explanation:

Option 1: pkill -f scan_filesystem
- This line sends the TERM signal to all processes named "scan_filesystem".
- pkill is used to send signals to processes, and the -f option tells pkill to match the entire command line of the processes.
- The * * * * * represents the time intervals for the cron job, indicating that the job will run every minute.

Option 2: pkill -u root -f scan_filesystem
- This option adds the -u root flag to restrict the search to processes owned by the root user.
- The rest of the command functions similarly to Option 1, sending the TERM signal to matching processes.

Option 3: pkill -u root -SIGKILL -f /path/to/scan_filesystem
- This option adds the -SIGKILL flag to forcefully terminate processes using the SIGKILL signal if graceful shutdown is not a concern.
- The rest of the command is similar to Option 2, with the addition of specifying the full path to the executable /path/to/scan_filesystem.

Question 8: User and
Group Management

Perform the following operations:

1. Establish the Admins Group, create an Admins directory in the /home directory, and assign ownership of the directory to the Admins group.
2. Create a group called "Developers."
3. Create a new user account with a username Sam, add the user to the Developers group, and set the home directory to /home/developers/Sam.
4. Assuming having a locked user account named "sysadmin". Troubleshoot and repair the user account to ensure successful password-based login.
5. Create a user account named "devops" with the default shell set to Bash.

Explanation

1. Establish the Admins Group, create an Admins directory, assign ownership:
```
$ sudo groupadd Admins
$ sudo mkdir /home/Admins
$ sudo chown :Admins /home/Admins
```

> sudo groupadd Admins: This command creates a new group called "Admins".
> sudo mkdir /home/Admins: This command creates a new directory called "Admins" in the /home directory.
> sudo chown :Admins /home/Admins: This command changes the ownership of the /home/Admins directory to the "Admins" group.

2. Create a group called "Developers":
$ sudo groupadd Developers

> sudo groupadd Developers: This command creates a new group called "Developers".

3. Create a new user account with specified attributes:
$ sudo useradd -m -d /home/developers/Sam -G Developers Sam

This command creates a new user called "Sam", adds the user to the "Developers" group, and sets the home directory to /home/developers/Sam.

4. Troubleshoot and repair the "sysadmin" user account for successful password-based login:
$ sudo passwd -u sysadmin

This command unlocks the "sysadmin" user account, allowing for successful password-based login.

5. Modify the default shell for the "devops" user account to Bash:
$ sudo usermod -s /bin/bash devops

This command changes the default shell for the "devops" user to Bash.

Explanation:

- Each command is executed with sudo to ensure it runs with administrative privileges.
- groupadd is used to create new groups, while useradd is used to create new user accounts.
- mkdir creates directories, and chown changes the ownership of files and directories.

- passwd -u unlocks a user account, allowing password-based login.
- usermod -s modifies user account attributes, in this case, changing the default shell.

Question 9: Automation and Configuration Management

Create a user account named 'automation' with passwordless sudo privileges.

Explanation

1. Create a new user named 'automation':
$ sudo useradd -m automation

This command creates a new user named 'automation' with the -m option telling useradd to create a home directory for the user.

2. Set passwordless sudo privileges for the 'automation' user:
$ echo "automation ALL=(ALL) NOPASSWD:ALL" | sudo tee / etc/sudoers.d/automation

This command adds a new rule to the sudoers file that allows the 'automation' user to run any command with sudo without being prompted for a password.
The echo command outputs the rule, and the tee command writes the rule to a new file in the /etc/sudoers.d directory.
The NOPASSWD:ALL part of the rule is what allows passwordless sudo access.

Explanation:

- Each command is executed with sudo to ensure it runs with administrative privileges.
- useradd is used to create a new user account, and the -m option ensures that a home directory is created for the user.
- The echo command is used to output the sudoers rule

allowing passwordless sudo access for the 'automation' user.

- tee is used to write the output of echo to a file, /etc/sudoers.d/automation, which is included in the sudoers configuration.

- The NOPASSWD:ALL part of the sudoers rule specifies that the 'automation' user can run any command with sudo without being prompted for a password.

Question 10: Special Permissions

Apply the sticky bit special permission to the directory located at /opt/shared/. Once done, ensure the correct setting of the sticky bit.

Explanation

# Apply the sticky bit
$ sudo chmod +t /opt/shared/

# Verify the sticky bit
$ ls -ld /opt/shared/

Explanation:

- The chmod +t command is employed to set the sticky bit on a directory. This permission safeguards the files within the directory, allowing only the file's owner, the directory's owner, or the root user to rename or delete the file. Other users, although possessing write permission for the directory, can only alter files they own.
- To confirm the application of the sticky bit, we utilize ls -ld. The presence of a 't' in the final position of the permissions string indicates the successful setting of the sticky bit."

Question 11: System Monitoring and User Management

Task:

Part 1: Create a command named ACC that allows all users to view a list of users who have previously logged into the system. The command should display the username, login time, and the terminal from which they logged in.

Part 2: The sysadmin user account is currently unable to log in using password authentication. Troubleshoot and repair the sysadmin user account to enable successful password-based login.

Explanation

Part 1: Create a command named ACC:

To create a command named ACC that lists all users who have previously logged into the system, the last command can be used. The last command reads from the /var/log/wtmp file, which records all logins and logouts.

Here's a simple script to achieve this:

```
#!/bin/bash
last
```

To make this script accessible as the command ACC:

- Save it to a file named ACC.
- Make it executable with chmod +x ACC.
- Move it to /usr/local/bin or any other directory in your PATH.

Part 2: Troubleshoot and Repair the sysadmin User Account:

If the sysadmin user account is unable to log in, it could be due to various reasons. Here are some steps to troubleshoot and repair the account:

Check if the account is locked:
```
$ passwd -S sysadmin
```

If the account is locked, unlock it with:
```
$ sudo passwd -u sysadmin
```

Check if the user's shell is valid: Check the sysadmin entry in the passwd file in the /etc directory. If the shell is not valid, change it with:
```
$ sudo chsh -s /bin/bash sysadmin
```

Check if the user's home directory exists and has correct permissions:
```
$ ls -ld /home/sysadmin
```

If the home directory does not exist or has incorrect permissions, create it or change its permissions with:
```
$ sudo mkdir /home/sysadmin
$ sudo chown sysadmin:sysadmin /home/sysadmin
```

If none of the above steps work, the user's password may be the issue. Change the password with:
```
$ sudo passwd sysadmin
```

Explanation:

- Part 1: The script uses the last command to display the login history of users. By making the script executable and placing it in a directory in the PATH, it becomes accessible as the command ACC.

- Part 2: Various issues could prevent the sysadmin user account from logging in. The steps provided help troubleshoot common issues such as locked accounts, invalid shells, incorrect permissions on the home directory, and password-related problems. Following these steps ensures that the sysadmin user account can successfully log in using password authentication.

Question 12: Networking and Basic Security

As the administrator of a small company server, you are tasked with configuring the network settings, hostname resolution, and time synchronization. You need to ensure that both IPv4 and IPv6 addresses are properly configured, along with DNS resolution through both DNS servers and the local hosts file. Additionally, the server must synchronize its time using NTP (Network Time Protocol). Below are the required configurations:

IPv4 Configuration:
IPv4 Address: 192.168.1.100
Netmask: 255.255.255.0
Gateway IP: 192.168.1.1
DNS IP: 8.8.8.8

IPv6 Configuration:
IPv6 Address: 2001:db8::100
Netmask: 64
Gateway IP: 2001:db8::1
DNS IP: 2001:4860:4860::8888

Explanation

1. Network Configuration:

IPv4 Configuration:
Identify the network interface to be configured. This can typically be found using the ip or ifconfig commands. For example, if the interface name is eth0, proceed with configuring it.

Set the IPv4 address using the ip addr add command:
```
$ ip addr add 192.168.1.100/24 dev eth0
```

Set the default gateway:
```
$ ip route add default via 192.168.1.1
```

Verify the configuration using:
```
$ ip addr show eth0
$ ip route show
```

2. IPv6 Configuration:

Assign the IPv6 address:
```
$ ip addr add 2001:db8::100/64 dev eth0
```

Add the default gateway for IPv6:
```
$ ip -6 route add default via 2001:db8::1
```

Verify the IPv6 configuration:
```
$ ip -6 addr show eth0
$ ip -6 route show
```

3. Hostname Resolution:

Edit the hosts file in the /etc/ directory to include the server's hostname and IP addresses:
```
$ sudo nano /etc/hosts
```

Add the following line:
```
192.168.1.100  servername
```

4. Configure DNS resolution by editing /etc/resolv.conf:
```
$ sudo nano /etc/resolv.conf
```

Add the following line:
```
server 8.8.8.8
```

5. Time Synchronization (NTP):

Install NTP daemon if not already installed:
```
$ sudo apt-get install ntp   # for Debian/Ubuntu
$ sudo yum install ntp       # for CentOS/RHEL
```

Edit the NTP configuration file /etc/ntp.conf:
```
$ sudo nano /etc/ntp.conf
```

Ensure the configuration includes NTP servers. Add or modify the following lines:
```
server 0.pool.ntp.org
server 1.pool.ntp.org
```

Restart the NTP service to apply changes:
```
$ sudo systemctl restart ntp
```

Verify the NTP synchronization status:
```
$ sudo ntpq -p
```

Question 13: Storage Management

Task:

Part 1: A swap partition /dev/sdb1 is currently configured to auto-attach at boot. Modify the system configuration to prevent this swap partition from auto-attaching at boot. Ensure that this configuration change does not affect the ability to manually mount the swap partition when needed.

Part 2: A physical volume /dev/sdc1 exists on the system. Your task is to create a volume group named myvg on this physical volume. Then, create a logical volume named mylv with a size of 2G on this volume group. Ensure that the logical volume is formatted with the ext4 filesystem and can be manually mounted to the /mnt/mylv directory.

Explanation

Part 1 Answer:

To prevent the swap partition /dev/sdb1 from auto-attaching at boot, you need to remove its entry from the /etc/fstab file. This file contains static information about the filesystems to be mounted automatically at boot time. Follow these steps:

- Open the /etc/fstab file in a text editor such as vi or nano.
- Locate the line corresponding to /dev/sdb1.
- Comment out the line by adding a # at the beginning of the line.

Save and exit the editor.

Part 2 Answer:

To create and manage a logical volume, you can use the Logical Volume Manager (LVM) tool. Follow these steps:

Create a physical volume on /dev/sdc1 using the pvcreate command:
`$ sudo pvcreate /dev/sdc1`

Create a volume group named myvg using the vgcreate command:
`$ sudo vgcreate myvg /dev/sdc1`

Create a logical volume named mylv with a size of 2G on myvg using the lvcreate command:
`$ sudo lvcreate -L 2G -n mylv myvg`

Format the logical volume with the ext4 filesystem using the mkfs command:
`$ sudo mkfs.ext4 /dev/myvg/mylv`

Create a mount point for the logical volume:
`$ sudo mkdir /mnt/mylv`

Mount the logical volume to the mount point:
`$ sudo mount /dev/myvg/mylv /mnt/mylv`

These steps ensure the creation of a logical volume with the ext4 filesystem on the /dev/sdc1 physical volume, enabling manual mounting to the /mnt/mylv directory.

Question 14: Filesystem Configuration

Assuming you have a filesystem at /dev/sdb1 that you want to use as a backup, configure the system for persistent read-only mounting of this filesystem at the /backup directory. Ensure that the filesystem is automatically mounted at boot time.

Explanation

To achieve this, follow these steps:

1. Begin by creating the mount point if it doesn't already exist:
$ sudo mkdir -p /backup

2. Now, open the /etc/fstab file with root privileges:
$ sudo nano /etc/fstab

3. Append the following line to the end of the file:
/dev/sdb1 /backup auto ro 0 0
This line directs the system to mount the filesystem at /dev/sdb1 to the /backup directory with read-only permissions (ro). The auto option instructs the system to determine the filesystem type automatically.

4. Save and exit the file.

5. To confirm there are no errors in the /etc/fstab file, execute the following command, which will attempt to mount all filesystems listed in /etc/fstab:
$ sudo mount -a

If successful, the filesystem should now be mounted read-only at /backup.

6. To verify the mount options, use the mount command:

```
$ mount | grep /backup
```

You should observe ro among the mount options for /backup.

Remember, this configuration persists across reboots due to its inclusion in the /etc/fstab file.

Question 15: Archives and Compression

You have a directory named /data that contains various files and subdirectories. Perform the following archive and compression operations using this directory:

1. Create a tarball of the /data directory.
2. Compress the tarball using gzip.
3. Decompress the gzip file and extract the tarball into a directory named /extracted.
4. Create a bzip2 compressed tarball of the /data directory.
5. Decompress the bzip2 file and extract the tarball into a directory named /extracted_bzip.

Explanation

Here are the steps to accomplish the tasks:

1. To create a tarball of the /data directory:
`$ tar -cvf data.tar /data`

2. To compress the tarball using gzip:
`$ gzip data.tar`
This generates a file named data.tar.gz.

3. To decompress the gzip file and extract the tarball into a directory named /extracted:
`$ mkdir /extracted`
`$ tar -xvzf data.tar.gz -C /extracted`

4. To create a bzip2 compressed tarball of the /data directory:
`$ tar -cvjf data.tar.bz2 /data`
This creates a file named data.tar.bz2.

5. To decompress the bzip2 file and extract the tarball into a directory named /extracted_bzip:

```
$ mkdir /extracted_bzip
$ tar -xvjf data.tar.bz2 -C /extracted_bzip
```

Remember, the -c option in the tar command is used to create a new archive, the -x option is used to extract files from an archive, the -v option is used for verbose listing of the files processed, the -f option allows you to specify the name of the archive, and the -z and -j options are used for gzip and bzip2 compression respectively. The -C option specifies the directory to extract the files.

Question 16: File Operations

Assuming you have a directory named /data that contains various files and subdirectories, perform the following file operations and provide the corresponding commands:

1. Locate all text files larger than 10MB in the /data directory.
2. Delete all empty files and directories within the /data directory.
3. Copy all .bak files from the /data directory to a new directory named /backup.
4. Move all files larger than 10MB from the /data directory to a new directory named /largefiles.
5. Rename a file named oldfile.txt in the /data directory to newfile.txt.
6. Create a symbolic link named linkfile.txt to a file named realfile.txt in the /data directory.
7. Display the contents of a file named file.txt in the /data directory.
8. Display and modify the permissions of a file named securefile.txt in the /data directory to rwxr-----.
9. Modify the ownership of a file named ownedfile.txt in the /data directory to the user user1 and the group group1.

Explanation

Here are the commands for each operation:

1. To locate all text files larger than 10MB in the /data directory:
```
$ find /data -type f -name "*.txt" -size +10M
```

2. To delete all empty files and directories within the /data directory:

```
$ find /data -type d -empty -delete
$ find /data -type f -empty -delete
```

3. To copy all .bak files from the /data directory to a new directory named /backup:

```
$ mkdir /backup
$ find /data -type f -name "*.bak" -exec cp {} /backup \;
```

4. To move all files larger than 10MB from the /data directory to a new directory named /largefiles:

```
$ mkdir /largefiles
$ find /data -type f -size +10M -exec mv {} /largefiles \;
```

5. To rename a file named oldfile.txt to newfile.txt in the /data directory:

```
$ mv /data/oldfile.txt /data/newfile.txt
```

6. To create a symbolic link named linkfile.txt to realfile.txt in the /data directory:

```
$ ln -s /data/realfile.txt /data/linkfile.txt
```

7. To display the contents of a file named file.txt in the /data directory:

```
$ cat /data/file.txt
```

8. To display and modify the permissions of a file named securefile.txt in the /data directory to rwxr-----:

```
$ ls -l /data/securefile.txt
$ chmod 740 /data/securefile.txt
```

9. To modify the ownership of a file named ownedfile.txt in the /data directory to the user user1 and the group group1:

```
$ chown user1:group1 /data/ownedfile.txt
```

Question 17: Kernel and Process Management

Using the specified tools, perform the following tasks:

1. Kernel Parameter Configuration: Use sysctl to display the value of the vm.swappiness kernel parameter. Then, change its value to 10.
2. Process Management: Use ps, top, kill, pkill, and pstree to:

- List all the running processes.
- Display real-time system status.
- Terminate a process with a specific PID.
- Terminate all processes with a specific name.
- Display the process tree of the system.

3. Service Management: Use systemctl, service, and update-rc.d to:

- Start, stop, and check the status of the sshd service.
- Enable the sshd service to start at boot time.

Explanation

1. Kernel Parameter Configuration:

Display the current value of the vm.swappiness kernel parameter:
```
$ sudo sysctl vm.swappiness
```

Change its value to 10:
```
$ sudo sysctl -w vm.swappiness=10
```

2. Process Management:

List all running processes:
`$ ps aux`

Display real-time system status:
`$ top`

Terminate a process using a specific PID (replace PID with the actual process ID):
`$ kill PID`

Terminate all processes with a specific name (replace processname with the actual process name):
`$ pkill processname`

Display the process tree of the system:
`$ pstree`

3. Service Management:

Start the sshd service:
`$ sudo systemctl start sshd`

Stop the sshd service:
`$ sudo systemctl stop sshd`

Check the status of the sshd service:
`$ sudo systemctl status sshd`

Enable the sshd service:
`$ sudo systemctl enable sshd`

For Ubuntu, use update-rc.d to enable or disable services. On CentOS, employ chkconfig or systemctl. To enable the sshd service to start at boot time using update-rc.d on Ubuntu:
`$ sudo update-rc.d sshd defaults`

Question 18: Essential Commands

Perform the following tasks:

1. Basic Git Operations:

Assuming you have a Git repository at /data/repo, perform the following operations:

- Initialize a new Git repository.
- Create a new file named file.txt, add some content to it, and commit it to the repository.
- Create a new branch named feature, switch to it, modify file.txt, and commit the changes.
- Switch back to the master branch and merge the feature branch into it.

2. Service Management:

Assuming you have a service named httpd, perform the following operations:

- Start the service.
- Check the status of the service.
- Stop the service.
- Configure the service to start at boot time.
- Troubleshoot the service if it fails to start.

Explanation

1. Basic Git Operations:

Initialize a new Git repository:
```
$ cd /data/repo
```

```
$ git init
```

Create a new file named file.txt, add content to it, and commit it to the repository:
```
$ echo "Hello, World!" > file.txt
$ git add file.txt
$ git commit -m "Add file.txt"
```

Create a new branch named feature, switch to it, modify file.txt, and commit the changes:
```
$ git checkout -b feature
$ echo "Hello, Git!" >> file.txt
$ git commit -am "Modify file.txt"
```

Switch back to the master branch and merge the feature branch into it:
```
$ git checkout master
$ git merge feature
```

2. Service Management:

Start the service:
```
$ sudo systemctl start httpd
```

Check the status of the service:
```
$ sudo systemctl status httpd
```

Stop the service:
```
$ sudo systemctl stop httpd
```

Configure the service to start at boot time:
```
$ sudo systemctl enable httpd
```

Troubleshoot the service if it fails to start:
```
$ journalctl -u httpd
```
This command will display system logs for the httpd service,

aiding in identifying any issues preventing its startup.

Question 19: System Recovery

You've encountered a scenario where you need to recover from various types of failures - hardware, operating system, or filesystem. The tasks include:

1. Hardware Failure Recovery:

- Identify hardware failures.
- Utilize system logs (/var/log/messages, /var/log/dmesg) to diagnose hardware issues.

2. Operating System Failure Recovery:

- Access recovery mode via the GRUB menu.
- Repair or reinstall broken packages.

3. Filesystem Failure Recovery:

- Diagnose and repair filesystem issues.
- Remount the root filesystem as read-write.

Explanation

1. Hardware Failure Recovery:

Identifying Hardware Failures:

Utilize hardware diagnostic tools such as lshw, lscpu, and lsblk to identify hardware failures. Example commands:

```
$ sudo lshw
$ sudo lscpu
$ sudo lsblk
```

Diagnosing Hardware Issues with System Logs:

Examine system logs /var/log/messages and /var/log/dmesg to detect hardware-related errors and warnings. Example commands:
```
$ sudo less /var/log/messages
$ sudo less /var/log/dmesg
```

2. Operating System Failure Recovery:

Accessing Recovery Mode via GRUB:

- Reboot the system and access the GRUB menu by pressing and holding the Shift key during boot.
- Select the 'Advanced options for Ubuntu/CentOS' submenu and choose the 'Recovery mode' option.

Repairing or Reinstalling Broken Packages:

Utilize package management tools such as apt for Ubuntu and dnf for CentOS to repair or reinstall broken packages. Example commands:

```
# Ubuntu 20.04
$ sudo apt update
$ sudo apt install --reinstall <package_name>
```

```
# CentOS Stream 8
$ sudo dnf reinstall <package_name>
```

3. Filesystem Failure Recovery:

Diagnosing and Repairing Filesystem Issues:

Use filesystem checking tools like fsck to diagnose and repair filesystem issues. Example command:

```
$ sudo fsck /dev/sdX
```

Remounting Root Filesystem as Read-Write:

Remount the root filesystem as read-write to perform repairs or modifications using the mount command. Example command:

```
$ sudo mount -o remount,rw /
```

Question 20: Container Configuration and Management

Task: As a system administrator, you are tasked with various Docker and container-related operations. Your tasks include:

1. Installation: Install Docker.
2. Container Creation: Create a Docker container named "web_server" based on the official nginx image with port 80 exposed to the host system.
3. Inspection: Retrieve detailed information about the "web_server" container, including its IP address, ports, and configuration.
4. Resource Management: Assign specific CPU and memory limits to the "web_server" container.
5. Log Retrieval: Fetch and view the logs of the "web_server" container.
6. Container Removal: Delete the "web_server" container from the system.
7. Docker Registry Interaction: Push the locally created "web_server" image to a private Docker registry accessible only to authorized users.
8. Container Backup and Restore: Back up the data within a Docker volume used by the "web_server" container and restore it to a new container.
9. Docker Usage: Showcase common Docker commands for managing containers, such as starting, stopping, and restarting.

Explanation

1. Installation:

Ubuntu 20.04:

```
$ sudo apt update
$ sudo apt install docker.io
```

CentOS Stream 8:
```
$ sudo dnf install docker
```

2. Container Creation:
```
$ sudo docker run -d --name web_server -p 80:80 nginx
```

3. Inspection:
```
$ sudo docker inspect web_server
```

4. Resource Management:
```
$ sudo docker update --memory="512m" --cpus="0.5" web_server
```

5. Log Retrieval:
```
$ sudo docker logs web_server
```

6. Container Removal:
```
$ sudo docker rm -f web_server
```

7. Docker Registry Interaction:

Tag the image:
```
$ sudo docker tag web_server username/repository:tag
```

Push to a private registry:
```
$ sudo docker push username/repository:tag
```

8. Container Backup and Restore:

Backup:
```
$ sudo docker run --rm -v container_volume:/volume -v $(pwd):/backup ubuntu tar cvf /backup/backup.tar /volume
```

Restore:
```
$ sudo docker run --rm -v container_volume:/volume -v $
(pwd):/backup ubuntu tar xvf /backup/backup.tar -C /volume
```

9. Docker Usage:

Starting a container:
```
$ sudo docker start web_server
```

Stopping a container:
```
$ sudo docker stop web_server
```

Restarting a container:
```
$ sudo docker restart web_server
```

Question 21: File Operations

Task: In your home directory, perform the following tasks on the file /home/tom/personal_info.txt:

1. Create a hard link to the file /opt/personal_info.txt with /home/tom/personal_info.txt. Confirm the creation of the hard link.
2. Create a soft link at /opt/softlink that points to the file at /home/tom/personal_info.txt. Ensure the soft link points to the absolute path, /home/tom/personal_info.txt, rather than a relative one. Confirm the creation of the soft link.

Explanation

1. Creating a hard link
# Use the ln command to create a hard link
$ sudo ln /home/tom/personal_info.txt /opt/personal_info.txt

# Verify the hard link creation
$ ls -li /home/tom/personal_info.txt /opt/personal_info.txt

2. Creating a soft link
# Use the ln -s command to create a soft link
$ sudo ln -s /home/tom/personal_info.txt /opt/softlink

Verify the soft link creation
$ ls -l /opt/softlink

Explanation:

- The ln command is utilized to create a hard link, requiring two arguments: the original file and the new link.

- To create a soft link, we utilize the ln -s command.
- Verification of the hard link is conducted using ls -li, displaying the files with their inode numbers. Matching inode numbers indicate a successful hard link.
- To verify the soft link, we use ls -l, which showcases the file the link points to.

Question 22: Network Configuration and Management

Task: On ServerA, configure a NetworkManager connection profile named "myprofile1" for the enp0s3 device with the following static settings. Ensure that the configuration is persistent across reboots. Additionally, verify the configuration by pinging an external server (e.g., google.com) after applying the settings.

- Static IPv4 Address: 192.168.1.2/24
- Static IPv6 Address: fd01::101/64
- IPv4 Default Gateway: 192.168.1.1
- IPv6 Default Gateway: fd01::100
- IPv4 DNS Servers: 8.8.8.8, 8.8.4.4
- IPv6 DNS Server: fd01::111
- DNS Search Domain: example.com

Explanation

1. To accomplish the specified task across both Debian and Fedora systems, execute the following commands:

Create the connection profile
```
$ nmcli connection add con-name myprofile1 type ethernet ifname enp0s3 ipv4.method manual ipv4.addresses 192.168.1.2/24 ipv4.gateway 192.168.1.1 ipv4.dns "8.8.8.8 8.8.4.4" ipv6.method manual ipv6.addresses fd01::101/64 ipv6.gateway fd01::100 ipv6.dns fd01::111 ipv4.dns-search example.com
```

Activate the connection
```
$ nmcli connection up myprofile1
```

The connection add command initializes a new connection profile with the specified parameters, while connection up activates the connection, applying the settings to the designated network interface.

For persistence across reboots, NetworkManager automatically preserves the connection profile in a file within /etc/NetworkManager/system-connections/.

2. To validate the configuration, ping an external server:
```
$ ping -c 4 google.com
```

This command dispatches four ICMP echo requests to google.com. Successful echo replies confirm the correctness of the network configuration. Conversely, any error or absence of replies suggests potential issues with the network configuration or connectivity. In such cases, review the connection profile settings and assess the status of the network interface and NetworkManager service.

Question 23: Advanced Network Configuration

Task: On ServerA, add the following secondary IPv4 address statically to the existing connection profile named "myprofile1". Ensure that the addition of this secondary IP address does not disrupt the existing network settings. After applying the settings, verify the configuration by checking the IP address of the network interface. Also, ensure that the configuration is persistent across reboots.

Secondary IPv4 Address: 10.0.0.5/24

Explanation

1. To incorporate a secondary IPv4 address into the "myprofile1" connection profile across Debian and Fedora systems:

Add the secondary IPv4 address to the connection profile
```
$ nmcli connection modify myprofile1 +ipv4.addresses 10.0.0.5/24
```

Reload the connection to apply the changes
```
$ nmcli connection down myprofile1 && nmcli connection up myprofile1
```
The connection modify command facilitates adjustments to the connection profile, utilizing the "+" symbol before ipv4.addresses to signify the addition of the specified IP address as a secondary address, preserving existing configurations. Subsequently, executing connection down and connection up commands brings the connection offline and back online, respectively, effectively applying the modifications to the network interface.

2. To validate the configuration, employ the nmcli connection show myprofile1 command, which furnishes a comprehensive display of the connection profile settings, including the newly added secondary IP address.

Question 24: System Time and Timezone Configuration

Task: On ServerA, configure the system time to the "America/ New_York" timezone. Ensure that the configuration is persistent across reboots. After applying the settings, verify the configuration by displaying the current system time and timezone. If the system uses NTP for time synchronization, ensure that the timezone change does not affect the synchronization.

Explanation

1. To adjust the system time to the "America/New_York" timezone, applicable to both Debian and Fedora systems:

# Set the system timezone
$ sudo timedatectl set-timezone America/New_York
Executing the set-timezone command establishes the desired timezone for the system. Given that modifying system time and timezone necessitates administrative privileges, employing sudo with the command is essential, contingent upon user permissions.

2. To ascertain the correctness of the configuration, invoke the timedatectl command without any arguments, yielding an output showcasing the current system time and timezone:
$ timedatectl
Within the output, verify that "America/New_York" appears under the "Time zone" designation.

Question 25: Logical Volume Management and Filesystem Operations

Task: On ServerA, perform the following operations using the /dev/sdb disk:

1. Create a physical volume on /dev/sdb.
2. Create a 2GiB volume group named "myvg" using the physical volume.
3. Create a 500MiB logical volume named "mylv" inside the "myvg" volume group.
4. Format the "mylv" logical volume with the ext4 filesystem.
5. Mount the "mylv" logical volume persistently on the /mylv directory. Ensure the directory exists before mounting.
6. Extend the "mylv" logical volume by 500MiB.
7. Resize the ext4 filesystem on "mylv" to use the additional space.

Explanation

1. To accomplish these tasks:

```
# 1. Create a physical volume on /dev/sdb
$ sudo pvcreate /dev/sdb
```

```
# 2. Create a 2GiB volume group named "myvg"
$ sudo vgcreate myvg /dev/sdb -s 2G
```

```
# 3. Create a 500MiB logical volume named "mylv" inside the
"myvg" volume group
$ sudo lvcreate -L 500M -n mylv myvg
```

```
# 4. Format the "mylv" logical volume with the ext4 filesystem
```

```
$ sudo mkfs.ext4 /dev/myvg/mylv
```

5. Create the /mylv directory if it doesn't exist
```
$ sudo mkdir -p /mylv
```

6. Mount the "mylv" logical volume persistently on the /mylv directory
```
$ echo '/dev/myvg/mylv /mylv ext4 defaults 0 0' | sudo tee -a /etc/fstab
$ sudo mount -a
```

7. Extend the "mylv" logical volume by 500MiB
```
$ sudo lvextend -L +500M /dev/myvg/mylv
```

8. Resize the ext4 filesystem on "mylv" to use the additional space
```
$ sudo resize2fs /dev/myvg/mylv
```

Question 26: File Searching and Manipulation

Task: On ServerA, locate all files larger than 3MB within the "/etc" directory. Copy these files to a new directory "/find/3mfiles", ensuring that the directory structure is preserved. If the "/find/3mfiles" directory does not exist, create it. After copying the files, verify the operation by listing the contents of the "/find/3mfiles" directory.

Explanation

To execute this task:

```
# Create the /find/3mfiles directory if it doesn't exist
$ sudo mkdir -p /find/3mfiles
```

```
# Locate and copy all files larger than 3MB within the "/etc"
directory to "/find/3mfiles"
$ sudo find /etc -type f -size +3M -exec cp --parents '{}' /
find/3mfiles \;
```

```
# Verify the operation by listing the contents of the "/
find/3mfiles" directory
$ ls -lhR /find/3mfiles
```

Explanation:

- The find command searches for files within a directory hierarchy. The -type f option specifies that only files (not directories) should be considered. The -size +3M option filters files larger than 3MB.
- The -exec option is used to execute a command on each found file. In this case, cp --parents '{}' /find/3mfiles copies

each found file to the specified directory while preserving the directory structure.

- sudo is used to grant administrative privileges for operations that require them, such as creating directories and copying files.

- Finally, ls -lhR lists the contents of the specified directory (/find/3mfiles) recursively in a human-readable format.

Question 27: System Boot and
Kernel Messages Configuration

Task: On ServerA, ensure that boot messages are displayed, not silenced, for troubleshooting purposes. This should include kernel messages and other system service startup messages. After making the necessary changes, reboot the system to verify that the boot messages are indeed displayed.

Explanation

To configure the system to exhibit boot messages:

1. Edit the GRUB configuration file:
$ sudo nano /etc/default/grub

2. Locate the line starting with GRUB_CMDLINE_LINUX_DEFAULT and eliminate "quiet" from it. For instance:
GRUB_CMDLINE_LINUX_DEFAULT="quiet splash"

should be altered to:
GRUB_CMDLINE_LINUX_DEFAULT="splash"

3. Save the file and exit the editor.

4. Update GRUB:

On Debian-based systems:
$ sudo update-grub

On Fedora-based systems:
$ sudo grub2-mkconfig -o /boot/grub2/grub.cfg

5. Reboot the system to implement the changes and verify the display of boot messages:

```
$ sudo reboot
```

Question 28: Bash Scripting and Command Line Arguments

Task: On ServerA, create a Bash script named "/script.sh" that accepts exactly two arguments. When executed with two arguments, the script should output the second argument followed by the first argument. If the script is executed with fewer or more than two arguments, it should display an error message and exit. After creating the script, verify its functionality by executing it with two test arguments.

Explanation

1. Create the script file:
$ sudo nano /script.sh

2. Enter the following script content:

```bash
#!/bin/bash

# Check if the number of arguments is exactly 2
if [ $# -ne 2 ]; then
    echo "Error: Exactly two arguments are required."
    exit 1
fi

# Output the second argument followed by the first argument
echo $2 $1
```

3. Save the file and exit the editor.

4. Make the script executable:
$ sudo chmod +x /script.sh

5. Verify the script functionality:
`$ ./script.sh test1 test2`

You should observe "test2 test1" as the output.

Explanation:

- The #!/bin/bash line at the beginning denotes that the script should be executed using the Bash shell.
- The if [$# -ne 2]; then ... fi block ensures that the number of arguments ($#) is exactly 2; if not, it displays an error message and exits with a non-zero status code.
- The echo $2 $1 line prints the second argument ($2) followed by the first argument ($1).

Question 29: User Account Management and File Operations

Task: On ServerA, ensure that a file named "Congrats" is automatically added to the home directories of all new users created in the future. The "Congrats" file should contain a welcome message for the new user. After setting up the configuration, create a test user account to verify that the "Congrats" file is indeed created in the new user's home directory.

Explanation

To ensure that a "Congrats" file is added to the home directories of all future users, follow these steps:

1. Create the "Congrats" file in the /etc/skel directory:
```
$ echo 'Welcome to ServerA!' | sudo tee /etc/skel/Congrats
```
The echo command outputs the welcome message, and tee writes the message to the "Congrats" file. Administrative privileges are required to create files in the /etc/skel directory, thus the use of sudo with the command.

2. Create a test user account to validate the configuration:
```
$ sudo useradd -m testuser
```
The useradd -m command generates a new user account along with a corresponding home directory. The -m flag specifies the creation of a home directory for the user.

3. Verify that the "Congrats" file is present in the new user's home directory:
```
$ ls /home/testuser
```
The output should include "Congrats".

Question 30: User and Group Management, File Permissions and Ownership

Task: On a Linux server (ServerA), perform the following tasks:

1. Create two groups: admins and developers.
2. Create four users: amr and biko, who should be members of the admins group, and carlos and david, who should be members of the developers group.
3. Create two directories: /admins and /developers. The /admins directory should be owned by biko and only accessible to the owner and members of the admins group. Similarly, the /developers directory should be owned by carlos and only accessible to members of the developers group.
4. Configure the system such that any new files created in the /admins or /developers directories are owned by the respective group owner.
5. Ensure that only the creators of files in these directories are allowed to delete their files.

Explanation

1. Create the groups
$ sudo groupadd admins
$ sudo groupadd developers

2. Create the users and add them to the respective groups
$ sudo useradd -m -G admins amr
$ sudo useradd -m -G admins biko
$ sudo useradd -m -G developers carlos
$ sudo useradd -m -G developers david

3. Create the directories

```
$ sudo mkdir /admins
$ sudo mkdir /developers
```

4. Change the ownership of the directories
```
$ sudo chown biko:admins /admins
$ sudo chown carlos:developers /developers
```

5. Change the permissions of the directories
```
$ sudo chmod 770 /admins
$ sudo chmod 770 /developers
```

6. Set the group ID on the directories so files created within them are owned by the group
```
$ sudo chmod g+s /admins
$ sudo chmod g+s /developers
```

7. Set the sticky bit on the directories so only the file owner can delete their files
```
$ sudo chmod +t /admins
$ sudo chmod +t /developers
```

Question 31: File Archiving and Compression

Task: On a system named ServerA, running either a Debian or Fedora distribution, create a compressed tar archive file named "/root/local.tgz". This archive should contain the directory "/usr/local/" and all of its contents.

Explanation

Step 1: Create the compressed tar archive
$ sudo tar -czvf /root/local.tgz /usr/local/

Explanation of the command:
-c: create a new archive
-z: compress the archive with gzip
-v: verbosely list the files processed
-f: use archive file

Step 2: Verify the integrity of the archive
$ sudo tar -tzvf local.tgz

Explanation of the command:
-t: list the contents of an archive
-z: work on gzip compression automatically in function
-v: verbosely list the files processed
-f: use archive file

Explanation:

This sequence of commands creates a compressed tar archive named "local.tgz" in the /root directory on ServerA, containing all the contents of the /usr/local/ directory. The tar command uses options -czvf to create a compressed archive with gzip, and -tzvf to verify its integrity.

Question 32: Disk Partitioning and Swap Space Management

Task: On a system named ServerA, create a 200MB swap partition using the secondary disk /dev/sdb.

Explanation

Step 1: Create a new partition on /dev/sdb
# Use the fdisk command to create a new partition
$ sudo fdisk /dev/sdb

Follow the prompts to create a new partition.
Make sure to set the partition type to '82' for Linux swap / Solaris

Step 2: Format the new partition as swap
$ sudo mkswap /dev/sdb1

Step 3: Activate the swap partition
$ sudo swapon /dev/sdb1

Step 4: Verify the swap space
$ free -m

Step 5: Make the swap partition activate at boot
# Open the /etc/fstab file
$ sudo nano /etc/fstab

Add the following line to the end of the file
/dev/sdb1 swap swap defaults 0 0

Save and exit the file

Step 6: Reboot the system and verify the swap space

```
$ sudo reboot
$ free -m
```

Question 33: Secure Remote Administration

Task: Set up an SSH passwordless root remote login from ServerA to ServerB.

Explanation

Step 1: Generate a key pair on ServerA (if it doesn't already exist)
$ ssh-keygen -t rsa

Step 2: Copy the public key to ServerB
$ ssh-copy-id root@ServerB

This command will prompt for the root password on ServerB

Step 3: Test the passwordless SSH login
$ ssh root@ServerB

This command should log in to ServerB without prompting for a password

Question 34: System Security
- SSH Configuration

Task: On ServerA, enhance the SSH security by limiting the maximum number of login attempts to 2.

Explanation

The SSH configuration file needs to be modified to limit the maximum number of login attempts.

1. Edit SSH Configuration:
\# Open the SSH configuration file in a text editor
$ sudo nano /etc/ssh/sshd_config

2. Set Maximum Login Attempts:
\# Add or modify the following line in the file
MaxAuthTries 2

3. Save and Exit:

4. Restart SSH Service:
$ sudo systemctl restart ssh # Debian
$ sudo systemctl restart sshd # Fedora

Question 35: Shell Scripting
- Text Processing

Task: On ServerA, create a versatile and informative shell script named "/trim.sh" that effectively removes any occurrences of the vowels "a", "i", "e", "o", and "u" from all provided arguments, regardless of their order. Ensure the script is well-formatted, incorporates error handling, provides clear output, and adheres to best practices.

Explanation

1. Create the Script File:
# Use your preferred text editor to create the script:
$ sudo vim /trim.sh

Add the following content, ensuring proper formatting:

#!/bin/bash

Check if any arguments were provided:

if [[$# -eq 0]]; then

echo "Error: Please provide at least one argument to trim."

exit 1

fi

Process and trim each argument individually, preserving order:

for arg in "$@"; do

```
trimmed=$(echo "$arg" | tr -d aeiou)

echo "$trimmed"

done
```

2. Save and Exit:
Press Esc to switch to command mode. Type `:wq` followed by Enter to save and exit.

3. Make the Script Executable:
```
$ sudo chmod +x /trim.sh
```

4. Verify Functionality:
```
$ /trim.sh "Hello World" "This is a test"
```

The output should be:
```
Hll Wrld
Ths s tst
```

Question 36: File Archiving and Compression

Task: On ServerA, create a compressed archive of the "/usr/local/bin/" directory using tar and bzip2. Store the archive under "/home" with the filename "local-bin.tar.bz2". Verify the contents of the archive.

Explanation

1. Create the compressed archive with informative flags:
$ sudo tar cvfj /home/local-bin.tar.bz2 /usr/local/bin/

Explanation of flags:
- c: Create a new archive
- v: Verbose mode, display files as they're added
- f: Specify the archive filename
- j: Use bzip2 compression

2. Verify the archive's contents:
$ tar tfv /home/local-bin.tar.bz2

Explanation of flags:
- t: List the contents of the archive
- f: Specify the archive filename
- v: Verbose mode, display file details

LFCS PRACTICE
EXAM TWO

Question 1: Text Manipulation

1. Extract Line Range: Extract lines 10 to 20 from a text file named example.txt and save them to a new file named extracted_lines.txt.

2. Count and Display: Count the occurrences of the word "Linux" in the example.txt file and display the count.

3. In-place Editing: Replace the second occurrence of the word "server" with "host" in the 15th line of the example.txt file.

4. Concatenate and Display: Concatenate two text files named file1.txt and file2.txt, and display the combined contents on the terminal.

Explanation

Extract Line Range: To extract a range of lines from a file in Linux, you can utilize the sed command. Here's how:

```
$ sed -n '10,20p' example.txt > extracted_lines.txt
```

This command instructs sed to print only the lines in the range 10 to 20 from example.txt and then redirects the output to extracted_lines.txt.

Count and Display: Counting occurrences of a word in a file can be accomplished using the grep command with appropriate options. Here's the command:

```
$ grep -o -i "Linux" example.txt | wc -l
```

This command extracts all occurrences of "Linux" from example.txt, ignoring case, and then counts these occurrences.

In-place Editing: For in-place editing, you can utilize the sed command. Here's the command to replace the second occurrence of "server" with "host" in the 15th line of example.txt:

```
$ sed '15s/server/host/2' example.txt
```

This command tells sed to perform the specified replacement in the designated line and occurrence.

Concatenate and Display: To concatenate and display the contents of two text files, you can use the cat command. Here's how:

```
$ cat file1.txt file2.txt
```

This command concatenates the contents of file1.txt and file2.txt and displays the result on the terminal.

Question 2: Package Management

Package Installation: Install the nginx package on your system using the appropriate package manager for your distribution.

Verification: Verify the successful installation of the nginx package.

Service Management: Start the nginx service and enable it to start on boot.

Package Information: Display detailed information about the installed nginx package.

Explanation

1. Package Installation: The commands to install nginx vary depending on the distribution:

On Ubuntu 20.04, utilize the apt package manager:
```
$ sudo apt install nginx
```

On CentOS Stream 8, use the dnf package manager:
```
$ sudo dnf install nginx
```

2. Verification: Verify the installation by checking the version of nginx:
```
$ nginx -v
```

3. Service Management: To start the nginx service and enable it to start on boot:
```
$ sudo systemctl start nginx
$ sudo systemctl enable nginx
```

4. Package Information: Display detailed information about the installed nginx package:

On Ubuntu 20.04:
```
$ apt show nginx
```

On CentOS Stream 8:
```
$ dnf info nginx
```

Question 3: Cron Job Management Challenge

As a system administrator, your responsibilities include:

Cron Job Scheduling: Schedule a cron job that runs a script named ~/backup.sh every day at 2 AM.

Script Creation: Develop a script named ~/backup.sh that backs up the current user's home directory to the `/backup` directory.

Cron Job Verification: Confirm that the cron job has been accurately scheduled.

Cron Job Execution: Ensure the cron job executes successfully, and the ~/backup.sh script functions as intended.

Explanation

1. Cron Job Scheduling: To schedule a cron job, access the crontab file using the following command:
`$ crontab -e`
This opens the crontab file in the default text editor. Add the following line to schedule the backup.sh script to run daily at 2 AM:
`0 2 * * * ~/backup.sh`

Save and exit the file.

2. Script Creation: Below is a sample backup.sh script:
`#!/bin/bash`
`rsync -a ~ /backup`
The rsync -a command will recursively copy files from the

source directory to the backup directory while preserving symbolic links, file permissions, ownerships, and timestamps.

3. Cron Job Verification: To verify the correctness of the cron job scheduling, view the current user's crontab entries with:
`$ crontab -l`
This command should display the cron job you added.

4. Cron Job Execution: Ensure the cron job executes successfully by checking the contents of the backup directory after it runs. If the backup directory contains files from the source directory, then both the cron job and the backup.sh script are functioning correctly.

Question 4: User and Group Management Challenge

As a system administrator, perform the following tasks:

1. User Creation: Create a new user named "test" with a home directory at /home/testuser.
2. Add User to Group and Grant Sudo: Add the user "test" to the "developers" group and grant sudo privileges.
3. Create User with Specific Attributes: Generate a new user account with the following attributes:
Username: newuser
Home Directory: /home/newuser
Default Shell: /bin/zsh.
4. Modify User Account: Modify the user account "developer" to change the default shell to /usr/bin/bash.
5. Disable User Account: Disable the user account "tempuser" to prevent login access.
6. Change Password Policy: Modify the password policy to enforce a minimum length of 10 characters and require at least one uppercase letter and one digit.

Explanation

1. User Creation: To create the user "test" with a home directory at /home/testuser, use the useradd command:
```
$ sudo useradd -m -d /home/testuser test
```

2. Add User to Group and Grant Sudo: Add the user "test" to the "developers" group and grant sudo privileges using usermod and gpasswd commands:
```
$ sudo usermod -aG developers test
$ sudo usermod -aG sudo test
```

3. Create User with Specific Attributes: Generate a new user account named "newuser" with a specified home directory and default shell using the useradd command:
```
$ sudo useradd -m -d /home/newuser -s /bin/zsh newuser
```

4. Modify User Account: Modify the default shell for the user "developer" to /usr/bin/bash using the chsh command:
```
$ sudo chsh -s /usr/bin/bash developer
```

5. Disable User Account: Disable the user account "tempuser" to prevent login access with the usermod command:
```
$ sudo usermod -L tempuser
```

6. Change Password Policy: Modify the password policy by editing the /etc/pam.d/common-password file and adding the following line:
```
password   [success=1 default=ignore] pam_unix.so obscure use_authtok try_first_pass
```

Question 5: System Monitoring Challenge

Configure system logging to capture authentication-related events, ensuring that all login attempts, both successful and unsuccessful, are logged, including the username and the source IP address.

Explanation

Step 1: Edit the syslog configuration file
# The syslog configuration file controls logging settings. Open it using a text editor.
$ sudo nano /etc/rsyslog.conf # Ubuntu 20.04
$ sudo nano /etc/syslog.conf # CentOS Stream 8

Step 2: Add configuration to log authentication events
Append the following line at the end of the file to instruct the syslog daemon to log authentication events to /var/log/auth.log.
echo 'auth,authpriv.* /var/log/auth.log' >> /etc/rsyslog.conf # Ubuntu 20.04
echo 'auth,authpriv.* /var/log/auth.log' >> /etc/syslog.conf # CentOS Stream 8

Step 3: Restart the syslog service
# Restart the syslog service to apply the changes.
$ sudo systemctl restart rsyslog # Ubuntu 20.04
$ sudo systemctl restart syslog # CentOS Stream 8

Step 4: Test the setup
SSH into the server from another machine and then check the /var/log/auth.log file to verify that login attempts are logged.

```
$ cat /var/log/auth.log
```

Explanation:

- In Step 1, the syslog configuration file (/etc/rsyslog.conf for Ubuntu 20.04 and /etc/syslog.conf for CentOS Stream 8) is opened using a text editor. This file dictates logging settings for the syslog daemon.
- In Step 2, a line is added to the configuration file instructing the syslog daemon to log messages from the auth and authpriv facilities to /var/log/auth.log. These facilities handle security, authorization, and authentication-related events.
- Step 3 involves restarting the syslog service (rsyslog for Ubuntu 20.04 and syslog for CentOS Stream 8) to apply the changes made to the configuration file.
- Finally, in Step 4, the setup is tested by SSHing into the server from another machine. Afterward, the /var/log/auth.log file is checked to ensure that login attempts, along with the associated username and source IP address, are correctly logged.

Question 6: Networking Challenge

Tasks:

1. Identify and display information about the network interfaces on your system, including IP addresses, MAC addresses, and the status of each interface.

2. Ensure proper hostname resolution using the hosts file in the /etc/ directory. Add an entry for a new host with the IP address 192.168.1.10 and hostname ServerB.

3. Verify that the hostname resolution is working correctly by pinging ServerB from ServerA.

Note: Perform these tasks on a system with hostname: ServerA.

Explanation

Task 1
# To display network interfaces and their information, you can use the `ip` command:
$ ip addr show

Task 2
# To add an entry to the hosts file in the /etc/ directory, you can use a text editor like `nano`:
$ sudo nano /etc/hosts

Add the following line to the file:
192.168.1.10 ServerB
Save and exit the file.

Task 3
To verify the hostname resolution, you can use the `ping` command:

`$ ping -c 3 ServerB`

Explanation:

- The ip addr show command displays all network interfaces along with their associated information such as IP addresses, MAC addresses, and their current status (up or down).
- The hosts file is a simple text file that maps IP addresses to hostnames. This file is checked before DNS, so it can be used to override DNS or provide hostname resolution when DNS is not available.
- The ping command sends a network request to a specific hostname or IP address. If the hostname resolution is working correctly, you should see responses from the IP address associated with the hostname you are pinging.

Question 7: User and Privilege Management

Tasks:

1. Create a new user named "manager" on your system.
2. Configure sudo rules to allow this user to restart the Apache service without a password prompt.
3. Ensure that the "manager" user cannot perform any other administrative tasks without a password prompt.
4. Test your configuration by switching to the "manager" user and attempting to restart the Apache service.

Explanation

1. Create a new user named "manager" on your system.
`$ sudo adduser manager`
This command creates a new user named "manager". The sudo command is used to run the adduser command with root privileges.

2. Configure sudo rules to allow this user to restart the Apache service without a password prompt.

To do this, we need to edit the sudoers file using the visudo command. This command opens the sudoers file safely for editing.
`$ sudo visudo`

In the opened sudoers file, add the following line:
`manager ALL=(ALL) NOPASSWD: /usr/sbin/service apache2 restart`
This line allows the "manager" user to run the command /usr/sbin/service apache2 restart as any user (ALL=(ALL)) without

being prompted for a password (NOPASSWD:).

3. Ensure that the "manager" user cannot perform any other administrative tasks without a password prompt.

The line we added to the sudoers file only allows the "manager" user to run the specified command without a password. Any other command run with sudo will still prompt for a password.

4. Test your configuration by switching to the "manager" user and attempting to restart the Apache service.

First, switch to the "manager" user:
```
$ su - manager
```

Then, try to restart the Apache service:
```
$ sudo /usr/sbin/service apache2 restart
```
If the configuration is correct, the Apache service should restart without prompting for a password.

Question 8: Create gzip-compressed tar archive

Create a gzip-compressed tar archive of the directory ~/data and name it ~/backup.tar.gz. Ensure that the archive includes all files and subdirectories within ~/data. After creating the archive, move it to the ~/backups directory. If ~/backups doesn't exist, create it.

Explanation

# Create the gzip-compressed tar archive
$ tar -czvf ~/backup.tar.gz ~/data

# Create the ~/backups directory if it doesn't exist
$ mkdir -p ~/backups

# Move the archive to the ~/backups directory
$ mv ~/backup.tar.gz ~/backups

Explanation:

- The tar -czvf ~/backup.tar.gz ~/data command creates a gzip-compressed tar archive of the ~/data directory.
- The -c option tells tar to create a new archive.
- The -z option tells tar to gzip the archive.
- The -v option tells tar to verbosely list the files processed.
- The -f option tells tar to use the following argument (in this case, backup.tar.gz) as the filename of the archive.
- The mkdir -p ~/backups command creates the ~/backups directory if it doesn't already exist.
- The -p option tells mkdir to create parent directories as needed.
- The mv ~/backup.tar.gz ~/backups command moves the ~/

backup.tar.gz archive to the ~/backups directory.

Question 9: Troubleshooting
Complex System Issues

1. Disk Space Issues: Using the command line, identify and resolve issues related to low disk space on any filesystem. Provide the commands to check the current disk usage, identify large files or directories, and safely free up space.

2. Network Connectivity: Troubleshoot and resolve network connectivity issues preventing access to a web server on the same system. Ensure your solution includes steps to check the status of the network interfaces, the firewall rules, and the web server itself. Also, provide the commands to test network connectivity both from within the system and from another system on the same network.

Explanation

1. Disk Space Issues:
Check Disk Usage: Use the df command to display disk space usage:
```
$ df -h
```

Identify Large Files or Directories: Use the du command to find large files or directories:
```
$ du -sh /*
```

Free Up Space: Delete unnecessary files or directories cautiously to avoid system instability. Always ensure you understand the purpose of each file or directory before deletion.

2. Network Connectivity:
Check Network Interfaces: Use the ip command to examine

network interfaces:
```
$ ip addr show
```

Check Firewall Rules: On Ubuntu, use ufw; on CentOS, use firewall-cmd:

```
# Ubuntu
$ sudo ufw status
```

```
# CentOS
$ sudo firewall-cmd --list-all
```

Check Web Server Status: Use systemctl to inspect the web server's status:
```
$ sudo systemctl status apache2
```
Replace apache2 with your web server's name.

Test Network Connectivity (Within System): Use the curl command to send a request to the local web server:
```
$ curl localhost
```

Test Network Connectivity (From Another System): Use the ping command to test connectivity from another system:
```
$ ping <IP address>
```
Replace <IP address> with your system's IP address.

Question 10: Docker Container Configuration and Management

Tasks:

1. Install Docker via the command line.
2. Once installed, pull the latest Nginx image from Docker Hub.
3. Create a Docker container hosting an Nginx web server accessible on port 8080 of the host machine.
4. Ensure that the Nginx server is configured to serve a simple HTML page.

Explanation

1. Install Docker via the command line.
The installation of Docker varies depending on the Linux distribution. For a distribution-agnostic approach, you can use the convenience script provided by Docker:

```
$ curl -fsSL https://get.docker.com -o get-docker.sh
$ sudo sh get-docker.sh
```

2. Pull the latest Nginx image from Docker Hub.

```
$ sudo docker pull nginx:latest
```

3. Create a Docker container hosting an Nginx web server accessible on port 8080 of the host machine.

```
$ sudo docker run --name my-nginx -p 8080:80 -d nginx:latest
```

This command creates a new Docker container named "my-nginx", maps port 8080 of the host machine to port 80 of the container, and runs the container in the background (-d).

4. Ensure that the Nginx server is configured to serve a simple HTML page.

First, create a simple HTML file:

```
$ echo "<h1>Welcome to Nginx!</h1>" > index.html
```

Then, copy this file into the Docker container:

```
$ sudo docker cp index.html my-nginx:/usr/share/nginx/html
```

5. Provide commands to confirm the Docker container's proper functioning and the accessibility of the Nginx server.

You can use the curl command to access the Nginx server:

```
$ curl http://localhost:8080
```

If everything is working correctly, you should see the message "Welcome to Nginx!".

6. Demonstrate how to view the logs of the running Nginx container.

You can view the logs of the running Docker container using the docker logs command:

```
$ sudo docker logs my-nginx
```

This command displays the logs of the "my-nginx" container, which includes the access logs of the Nginx server.

Question 11: User Resource Management

As a system administrator, you're responsible for optimizing system performance and preventing resource hogging by individual users.

Tasks:

1. Limit Process Creation for Sarah: Define a hard limit for user Sarah, restricting her ability to open more than 25 processes simultaneously.

2. Verify Configuration: Confirm the successful application of the limit by checking Sarah's resource settings.

Explanation

1. Setting the Limit:
```
$ sudo echo "Sarah hard nproc 25" >> /etc/security/limits.conf
```

sudo: Required for administrative tasks.
echo: Used to create the line to be appended.
"Sarah hard nproc 25": Defines the limit for Sarah.
Sarah: Username for whom the limit applies.
hard: Sets a hard limit, the maximum allowed processes.
nproc: Specifies the resource being limited (number of processes).
25: The maximum number of processes allowed for Sarah.
>>: Appends the line to the specified file.
/etc/security/limits.conf: File defining user resource limits.

2. Verification:

```
$ sudo grep Sarah /etc/security/limits.conf
```

sudo: Required for administrative tasks.

grep Sarah /etc/security/limits.conf: Searches for lines containing "Sarah" in the limits.conf file. You should see the line "Sarah hard nproc 25".

limits.conf: This file defines resource limitations for users and groups.

Question 12: User Account
Security and Access Control

As part of your system administration duties, you need to manage user access for security and operational efficiency.

Tasks:

1. Lock admin1's Account: admin1 is going on vacation and won't need system access. Disable their login to prevent unauthorized access.

2. Unlock admin2's Account: admin2 is back from leave and requires system access. Re-enable their login for resumed work.

3. Verify Account Status: Confirm the success of your actions by attempting to log in as each user.

Explanation

1. Lock Account (admin1):
$ sudo passwd -l admin1

sudo: Required for administrative tasks.
passwd: Command to manage user passwords.
-l: Flag to lock the user account.
admin1: Username of the account to be locked.

2. Unlock Account (admin2):
$ sudo passwd -u admin2

passwd: Command to manage user passwords.
-u: Flag to unlock the user account.

admin2: Username of the account to be unlocked.

3. Verification:

- Attempt to switch to admin1 using *su - admin1*. A locked account will deny access.
- Attempt to switch to admin2 using *su - admin2*. A successful login indicates a properly unlocked account.

Explanation:

- The passwd command with the -l flag disables login for a user by adding an exclamation mark ("!") to their password entry in the shadow file.
- The passwd command with the -u flag removes the exclamation mark, allowing the user to log in again.

Question 13: Network
Interface Configuration

On a Linux server named ServerB, you are tasked with modifying the active network interface configuration to statically follow these specifications:

IPV4 Address: 192.168.1.3/24
Gateway (GW): 192.168.1.1
DNS Server: 8.8.8.8

Explanation

The task can be accomplished using the nmcli command-line tool or its text-based user interface alternative nmtui. Here are the steps for both methods:

Using nmcli:

1. Identify the active connection profile and device. For example, if the connection profile is "myprofile2" and the device is "enp0s3", use:
$ nmcli connection show --active

2. Set the IPV4 address:
$ nmcli connection modify myprofile2 ipv4.addresses 192.168.1.3/24

3. Set the gateway:
$ nmcli connection modify myprofile2 ipv4.gateway 192.168.1.1

4. Set the IPv4 method to manual (not DHCP):
$ nmcli connection modify myprofile2 ipv4.method manual

5. Configure DNS:
```
$ nmcli connection modify myprofile2 ipv4.dns 8.8.8.8
```

6. Restart the NetworkManager service:
```
$ systemctl restart NetworkManager
```

7. Reload NetworkManager configuration files without restarting the NetworkManager service:
```
$ nmcli con reload
```

8. Verify the new network configuration:
```
$ nmcli con sh myprofile2
```
or
```
$ ip address show enp0s3
```

Using nmtui:

1. Launch the text-based user interface:
```
$ nmtui
```

2. Select "Edit a connection".

3. Choose the interface you want to configure.

4. Select "Add" > "Ethernet", then add the IPv4 address, define the subnet mask, Gateway, and DNS servers.

5. After finishing your configuration, select "OK".

6. Select "Back".

7. Select "Activate a connection", then "OK".

8. Deactivate your interface name, then reactivate it.

9. Select "Back".

10. Select "Quit".

11. Verify the new configuration:
`$ ip ad sh interface_name`

Note: The nmcli and nmtui commands provide a command-line and a text-based user interface, respectively, for managing network settings on Linux. They are part of the NetworkManager utility, which is installed by default on most Linux distributions. Remember to replace "myprofile2" and "enp0s3" with your actual connection profile and device names. You can find these by running *nmcli connection show --active.*

Question 14: Adding a Secondary IP Address to a Network Interface

On a Linux server named ServerB, you are tasked with adding a secondary IPV4 address to your currently active network interface. The task should be accomplished in a way that doesn't affect the existing network settings. The secondary IPV4 address to be added is 10.0.0.3/24.

Explanation

The task can be accomplished using the nmcli command-line tool. Here are the steps:

1. Display the currently active network connections:
$ nmcli con sh --active

2. Modify an existing NetworkManager connection, for example "myprofile2", and add an IPv4 address of "10.0.0.3/24" to it:
$ nmcli con mod myprofile2 +ipv4.addresses 10.0.0.3/24

3. Reload NetworkManager configuration files without restarting the NetworkManager service:
$ nmcli connection reload

Or bring up the "myprofile2" network connection:
$ nmcli con up myprofile2

4. Verify the new network configuration. Display the details of the network device, for example "enpOs3":
$ nmcli dev sh enpOs3

Or display the details of the network connection profile named "myprofile2":

```
$ nmcli con sh myprofile2
```

Question 15: Configuring System Timezone

On a Linux server named ServerB, you are tasked with setting the system time to your nearest timezone.

Explanation

The task can be accomplished using the timedatectl command-line tool. Here are the steps:

1. View the current system clock and timezone settings:
```
$ timedatectl
```

2. List all available timezones:
```
$ timedatectl list-timezones
```

3. If you are specifically interested in timezones in Europe that start with "Europe/L", you can filter the list:
```
$ timedatectl list-timezones | grep -o "Europe/L.*"
```

4. Set the system's timezone to your nearest timezone. For example, to set it to "Europe/London", run:
```
$ timedatectl set-timezone "Europe/London"
```

5. Verify the new system timezone:
```
$ timedatectl
```

Question 16: Configuring Network Time Protocol (NTP) Synchronization

On a Linux server named ServerB, you are tasked with ensuring that NTP synchronization is configured. This involves setting up the system to synchronize its clock with a remote time server over a network.

Explanation

The task can be accomplished using the timedatectl and chrony tools. Here are the steps:

1. View the current system clock and timezone settings:
`$ timedatectl`

2. Install the chrony package, which provides NTP synchronization for the system clock:
`$ dnf install chrony -y`

3. Enable and start the Chrony service immediately:
`$ systemctl enable chronyd --now`

4. Display the contents of the chrony configuration file located at /etc/chrony.conf to check the configuration after installation:
`$ cat /etc/chrony.conf`

5. Enable automatic time synchronization with NTP servers:
`$ timedatectl set-ntp true`

6. Verify the NTP synchronization status:
`$ timedatectl`

Note:

- NTP is a protocol that allows a computer to synchronize its clock with a remote time server over a network. When NTP synchronization is enabled, the system clock is automatically adjusted to match the time reported by the NTP server. This can be useful for ensuring accurate timekeeping on a Linux system, which can be important for tasks such as logging, debugging, and authentication.
- Chrony is a software package that provides NTP synchronization for the system clock. It synchronizes the system clock with a reliable time source, such as an NTP server, to ensure that the clock is accurate and consistent. The chrony configuration file (/etc/chrony.conf) includes settings for NTP servers, time sources, allow and deny rules, and logging.

Question 17: Network Configuration and Management

Tasks:

- On a Linux server named ServerB, you are tasked with enabling IPV4 packet forwarding persistently. This involves setting up the system to forward packets from one network interface to another.

- Verify that the changes have been applied correctly and that packet forwarding is enabled.

Explanation

1. Enable IPV4 packet forwarding persistently.

To enable IPV4 packet forwarding persistently, you need to edit the /etc/sysctl.conf file. This file is used to configure kernel parameters at runtime.
$ sudo nano /etc/sysctl.conf

Add or uncomment the following line in the file:
net.ipv4.ip_forward=1
This line enables IPV4 packet forwarding.

2. Apply the changes.

After editing the /etc/sysctl.conf file, you need to apply the changes using the sysctl command:
$ sudo sysctl -p
This command loads the configuration data from /etc/sysctl.conf.

3. Verify that packet forwarding is enabled.

You can verify that packet forwarding is enabled by running the following command:
```
$ sysctl net.ipv4.ip_forward
```
If packet forwarding is enabled, this command will output net.ipv4.ip_forward = 1.

Implications and use cases of packet forwarding:

Enabling packet forwarding allows a Linux server to forward packets from one network interface to another, effectively allowing it to function as a router. This can be useful in various scenarios, such as when setting up a VPN server, configuring a firewall, or implementing network address translation (NAT).

Question 18: IPv6 Network Configuration and Troubleshooting

Tasks:

- On a system named ServerB, your task is to enable IPv6 packet forwarding. This configuration should persist even after a system reboot.

- Verify that the changes have been applied successfully.

Explanation

1. Enable IPv6 packet forwarding.

To enable IPv6 packet forwarding, you need to edit the /etc/sysctl.conf file. This file is used to configure kernel parameters at runtime.
`$ sudo nano /etc/sysctl.conf`

Add or uncomment the following line in the file:
`net.ipv6.conf.all.forwarding=1`
This line enables IPv6 packet forwarding.

2. Apply the changes.

After editing the /etc/sysctl.conf file, you need to apply the changes using the sysctl command:
`$ sudo sysctl -p`
This command loads the configuration data from /etc/sysctl.conf.

3. Verify that packet forwarding is enabled.

You can verify that packet forwarding is enabled by running the following command:

```
$ sysctl net.ipv6.conf.all.forwarding
```

If packet forwarding is enabled, this command will output net.ipv6.conf.all.forwarding = 1.

Implications and use cases of packet forwarding:

Enabling packet forwarding allows a Linux server to forward packets from one network interface to another, effectively allowing it to function as a router. This can be useful in various scenarios, such as when setting up a VPN server, configuring a firewall, or implementing network address translation (NAT).

Question 19: Linux System Boot Process and Troubleshooting

Tasks:

On a system named ServerB, ensure that boot messages are displayed during the system startup process and are not silenced. These changes should persist across reboots.

Explanation

1. Ensure that boot messages are displayed during the system startup process and are not silenced.

To ensure that boot messages are displayed during the system startup process, you need to edit the GRUB configuration file. GRUB is the bootloader used by most Linux distributions.
$ sudo nano /etc/default/grub

Find the line that starts with GRUB_CMDLINE_LINUX_DEFAULT and remove quiet from the list of options. The quiet option suppresses most boot messages.
GRUB_CMDLINE_LINUX_DEFAULT="splash"

2. Make the changes persist across reboots.

After editing the GRUB configuration file, you need to update GRUB to apply the changes:
$ sudo update-grub
This command generates a new GRUB configuration file based on the contents of /etc/default/grub and the scripts in /etc/grub.d.

3. Verify that the changes have been applied successfully.

You can verify that the changes have been applied successfully by rebooting your system:

```
$ sudo reboot
```

During the reboot, you should see boot messages displayed on the screen.

Question 20: Logical Volume Management and Filesystem Expansion

On a system named ServerB, perform the following tasks using the /dev/sdb disk:

1. Create a volume group named vgmyvg with a size of 4GiB.
2. Inside the vgmyvg volume group, create a logical volume named lvmylv with a size of 1GiB.
3. Format the lvmylv logical volume with the ext4 filesystem.
4. Mount the lvmylv logical volume persistently on the /lvmylv directory.
5. Extend the ext4 filesystem on lvmylv by 500M.
6. Verify that the filesystem has been successfully extended.

Explanation

Create a volume group named vgmyvg: Use the vgcreate command to create a new volume group named vgmyvg with /dev/sdb as the physical volume:
$ vgcreate vgmyvg /dev/sdb

Create a logical volume named lvmylv: Use the lvcreate command to create a new logical volume named lvmyvg with a size of 1GiB inside the vgmyvg volume group:
$ lvcreate -L 1G -n lvmylv vgmyvg

Format the lvmylv logical volume: Use the mkfs.ext4 command to format the lvmylv logical volume with the ext4 filesystem:
$ mkfs.ext4 /dev/vgmyvg/lvmylv

Mount the lvmylv logical volume: First, create the mount point directory /lvmylv if it doesn't exist. Then, use the mount command to mount the lvmylv logical volume on the /lvmylv directory:

```
$ mkdir -p /lvmylv
$ mount /dev/vgmyvg/lvmylv /lvmylv
```

To mount the volume persistently, add the following line to the /etc/fstab file:

```
/dev/vgmyvg/lvmylv /lvmylv ext4 defaults 0 0
```

Extend the ext4 filesystem on lvmylv: Use the lvextend command to extend the lvmylv logical volume by 500M, and the resize2fs command to resize the ext4 filesystem to occupy all the available space in the logical volume:

```
$ lvextend -L +500M /dev/vgmyvg/lvmylv
$ resize2fs /dev/vgmyvg/lvmylv
```

Verify the filesystem extension: Use the df -h command to display the size of the mounted filesystems. The size of the /lvmylv filesystem should now be 1.5GiB.

Question 21: Shell Scripting and Argument Handling

Tasks:

On a system named ServerB, write a script "~/yes-no.sh" that accepts one argument:

- If the argument is 'yes', the script should run the command echo "that's nice".
- If the argument is 'no', the script should run the command echo "I am sorry to hear that".
- If the argument is anything else, the script should run the command echo "unknown argument provided".
- If no argument is provided, the script should display a usage message and exit with a non-zero status code.
- Ensure that the script has the appropriate permissions to be executed.
- Test your script with various arguments and verify its behavior.

Explanation

1. Write the script "~/yes-no.sh".

Here's the content of the script:

```
#!/bin/bash

# Check if an argument was provided
if [ $# -eq 0 ]; then
  echo "Usage: $0 <yes|no>"
  exit 1
fi
```

```
# Handle the argument
case $1 in
  yes)
    echo "That's nice"
    ;;
  no)
    echo "I am sorry to hear that"
    ;;
  *)
    echo "Unknown argument provided"
    ;;
esac
```

This script first checks if an argument was provided ($# -eq 0). If not, it displays a usage message and exits with a non-zero status code. Then, it uses a case statement to handle the argument ($1).

2. Ensure that the script has the appropriate permissions to be executed.

You can use the chmod command to make the script executable:
```
$ chmod +x ~/yes-no.sh
```

3. Test the script with various arguments and verify its behavior.

You can test the script by running it with various arguments:
```
$ ~/yes-no.sh yes
$ ~/yes-no.sh no
$ ~/yes-no.sh maybe
$ ~/yes-no.sh
```
The script should behave as expected based on the provided argument.

Question 22: System Configuration and Hostname Management

Change the hostname to "Node5" and ensure that the change is persistent across reboots. Additionally, verify that the hostname has been correctly updated.

Explanation

You can use the hostnamectl command to change the hostname:

```
$ sudo hostnamectl set-hostname Node5
```

This change will be persistent across reboots. You can verify the change with:

```
$ hostnamectl
```

Question 23: Find

Find the regular files owned by the user root in the "/usr/bin" and copy the files into the "/find/rootfiles/" directory

Explanation

1. Directory Creation: To create a new directory named "rootfiles" within the "/find" directory, execute the following command:
`$ sudo mkdir -p /find/rootfiles`
The -p option ensures the creation of any non-existent parent directories.

2. File Search and Copy: To locate all files within the "/usr/bin" directory owned by the root user and copy them to the "/find/rootfiles" directory, execute the following command:
`$ sudo find /usr/bin/ -type f -user root -exec cp {} /find/rootfiles/ \;`

Here's a breakdown of the command:
find /usr/bin/: Initiates the search within the /usr/bin directory.
-type f: Restricts the search to regular files only.
-user root: Filters the results to include files owned solely by the root user.
-exec cp {} /find/rootfiles/ \;: Executes the cp command to copy each located file to the /find/rootfiles directory. # The {} is replaced with the name of each file found by the find command. The semicolon is escaped with a backslash, which is necessary to terminate the -exec command.

3. Directory Content Listing: To display the contents of the "/find/rootfiles/" directory in a detailed format, run the

following command:

```
$ sudo ls -l /find/rootfiles/
```

This command lists the files along with their permissions, number of links, owner, group, size, and time of last modification.

Question 24: User Account Management and Security

As a system administrator, you are required to manage user accounts on a Linux server. You have a user named Sam. Your task is to configure Sam's account in such a way that his password will expire after 100 days. Additionally, ensure that Sam is notified 7 days before his password expires so he can change it.

Explanation

1. To set the password to expire after 100 days, use the following command:
`$ sudo chage -M 100 Sam`
The -M option sets the maximum number of days during which the password is valid.

2. To set a warning for Sam 7 days before his password expires, use the following command:
`$ sudo chage -W 7 Sam`
The -W option sets the number of days of warning before a password expires.

3. To verify the changes, use the following command:
`$ sudo chage -l Sam`
This command displays the password and aging information for Sam's account.

Explanation:
- In Linux, the chage command is used to modify user password expiry information. It enables aging for the password, which ensures that the password will be changed from time to time for security reasons.

- The -M option is used to set the maximum number of days the password is valid.
- The -W option is used to set a warning period before the password expires.
- The chage -l command is used to check the password and aging information.

Question 25: Task Scheduling and Automation

As a system administrator, you are required to automate tasks on a Linux server. Your task is to create a cron job that runs as root and deletes empty files from the /tmp directory at 12:45 am daily.

Explanation

1. To edit the crontab for the root user, use the following command:
$ sudo crontab -e

2. Add the following line to the crontab file:
45 0 * * * find /tmp -type f -empty -delete
This line sets a cron job that runs the find command at 12:45 am daily. The find command searches the /tmp directory for empty files and deletes them.

3. Save and close the crontab file.

4. To verify the changes, use the following command:
$ sudo crontab -l
This command lists the cron jobs for the root user.

Explanation:
- In Linux, the crontab command is used to create, edit, install, uninstall, and list cron jobs. A cron job is a scheduled task that runs automatically at specified times. The - find command is used to search for files in a directory hierarchy. In this case, it's used to find and delete empty files in the /tmp directory.

Question 26: File Archiving and Compression

As a system administrator, you are required to manage file backups on a Linux server. Your task is to create a compressed tar file named "/archive/myetc.tbz2" of the "/etc" directory.

After creating the archive, you need to restore the archived data in the "/restored/myetc/" directory. Ensure that the original permissions and ownerships are preserved during the restoration process.

Explanation

1. To create a compressed tar file of the "/etc" directory, use the following command:
$ sudo tar -cjf /archive/myetc.tbz2 /etc
The -c option creates a new archive, -j option uses bzip2 for compression, and -f specifies the name of the archive file.

2. To restore the archived data in the "/restored/myetc/" directory, use the following command:
$ sudo mkdir -p /restored/myetc && sudo tar -xjf /archive/myetc.tbz2 -C /restored/myetc
The -x option extracts files from an archive, -j option decompresses the archive using bzip2, -f specifies the name of the archive file, and -C changes to directory DIR.

3. To verify the changes, use the following command:
$ ls -l /restored/myetc
This command lists the files in the restored directory.

Explanation:

In Linux, the tar command is used to create, maintain, modify, and extract files from an archive file known as a tarfile. A tarfile is often used to store and distribute a whole directory hierarchy of files. The tar command provides numerous options, such as -c for creating a new archive, -j for compression/decompression using bzip2, -f for specifying the name of the archive file, and -x for extracting files from an archive.

Question 27: Secure Shell (SSH) Configuration

On a Linux server named Node1, your task is to disable password authentication for SSH connections. Ensure that the change does not disrupt existing SSH connections. After completing the task, verify your configuration.

Explanation

1. Open the SSH daemon configuration file in a text editor. You might use vi, nano, or another text editor, depending on your preference:
$ sudo vi /etc/ssh/sshd_config

2. Find the line that contains #PasswordAuthentication yes, uncomment it by removing the # at the beginning of the line, and change yes to no so it looks like this:
PasswordAuthentication no

3. Save and close the file.

4. To ensure that your changes don't disrupt existing connections, you should reload the SSH daemon configuration instead of restarting it. Use the following command:
$ sudo systemctl reload sshd

5. To verify your configuration, you can use the following command:
$ grep PasswordAuthentication /etc/ssh/sshd_config
This command should return PasswordAuthentication no, confirming that password authentication has been disabled.

Question 28: Disk Partitioning and Swap Space Configuration

On a Linux server named Node2, your task is to create a 500MiB swap partition using the /dev/sdc disk. This swap space should be enabled automatically at boot time.

Explanation

1. Use fdisk to create a new partition on /dev/sdc:
```
$ sudo fdisk /dev/sdc
```
Then follow the prompts to create a new partition. Make sure to specify the size as 500MiB.

2. Once the partition is created (let's assume it's /dev/sdc1), set up the swap area:
```
$ sudo mkswap /dev/sdc1
```

3. Enable the swap space:
```
$ sudo swapon /dev/sdc1
```

4. To ensure the swap space is enabled automatically at boot, add an entry to the /etc/fstab file:
```
$ echo '/dev/sdc1 none swap sw 0 0' | sudo tee -a /etc/fstab
```

5. Verify that the swap space is active by using the free or swapon command:
```
$ free -h
```
or
```
$ swapon --show
```
These commands should show that /dev/sdc1 is being used as swap.

Question 29: Secure Shell
(SSH) Configuration

On a Linux server named Node1, your task is to restrict root login over SSH.

Explanation

1. Open the SSH daemon configuration file in a text editor. You might use vi, nano, or another text editor, depending on your preference:
$ sudo vi /etc/ssh/sshd_config

2. Find the line that contains #PermitRootLogin yes, uncomment it by removing the # at the beginning of the line, and change yes to no so it looks like this:
PermitRootLogin no

3. Save and close the file.

4. To ensure that your changes don't disrupt existing connections, you should reload the SSH daemon configuration instead of restarting it. Use the following command:
$ sudo systemctl reload sshd

5. To verify your configuration, you can use the following command:
$ grep PermitRootLogin /etc/ssh/sshd_config
This command should return PermitRootLogin no, confirming that root login has been restricted.

Question 30: Configuring Docker and Setting Up a Local Image Repository

Your task involves configuring a Linux server named Node1 for container management and image repository setup. Begin by installing the Docker package. Next, set up a local image repository within the /var/lib/registry directory, accessible on port 5000. After configuring the repository, pull the httpd container image from Docker Hub and push it to your local image repository.

Explanation

1. Install Docker: Begin by installing the Docker package on Node1. The installation process may vary slightly depending on the Linux distribution. Use the following commands to install Docker:

```
# Update package index
$ sudo apt update         # For Debian/Ubuntu
$ sudo yum update         # For CentOS/RHEL
```

```
# Install Docker package
$ sudo apt install docker.io   # For Debian/Ubuntu
$ sudo yum install docker      # For CentOS/RHEL
```
This command installs Docker along with its dependencies.

2. Set Up Local Image Repository: Create a local image repository directory and configure it to be accessible on port 5000. Execute the following commands:
```
$ sudo mkdir -p /var/lib/registry
$ sudo docker run -d -p 5000:5000 --restart=always --name registry -v /var/lib/registry:/var/lib/registry registry:2
```

These commands create a local image repository using the official Docker Registry image. The repository will be accessible on port 5000.

3. Pull and Push Container Images: Pull the httpd container image from Docker Hub and push it to your local image repository. Use the following commands:

```
# Pull the httpd container image from Docker Hub
$ sudo docker pull httpd
```

```
# Tag the pulled image for the local repository
$ sudo docker tag httpd localhost:5000/httpd
```

```
# Push the tagged image to the local repository
$ sudo docker push localhost:5000/httpd
```

These commands fetch the httpd container image from Docker Hub, tag it for your local repository (on port 5000), and then push it to the local repository.

4. Verify Repository and Image: To ensure that the local image repository has been set up successfully and the httpd container image has been pushed to it, you can list the images stored in the local repository. Execute:

```
$ sudo docker images
```

This command lists all the images available on the system. You should see the httpd image tagged as localhost:5000/httpd.

Question 31: Process Management
and Prioritization

On a Linux server, your task is to run the command sleep 100 in the background with a priority value of 30.

Explanation

1. Run the sleep 100 command in the background with a priority value of 30:
$ nice -n 30 sleep 100 &
The & at the end of the command runs the process in the background.

2. To verify that the process is running with the correct priority, you can use the ps command with the -l (long format) option, which includes the nice value in its output:
$ ps -l
Look for the sleep 100 command in the output. The NI column shows the nice value of each process. The sleep 100 command should have a nice value of 30.

Question 32: Process Management and Signal Handling

On a Linux server, your task is to terminate a process with the PID 112. However, the process should be allowed to "clean up" before exiting, meaning it should be given the opportunity to handle the termination signal and perform any necessary final tasks.

Explanation

To terminate a process while allowing it to clean up, you would typically send it the SIGTERM signal, which requests the process to terminate but allows it to catch the signal and perform cleanup tasks before exiting. Here are the steps:

1. Send the SIGTERM signal to the process with PID 112:
$ kill -SIGTERM 112

2. To verify that the process is no longer running, you can use the ps command:
$ ps -p 112
If the process is no longer running, this command will not return any output.

Question 33: File Redirection and Command Output

On a Linux server, your task is to execute the echo command with the argument cmd, and redirect its output to a file located at ~/cmd.txt. If the file already exists, it should be overwritten.

Explanation

To redirect the output of a command to a file, you would typically use the > operator, which overwrites the file if it already exists. Here are the steps:

1. Run the echo command with the argument cmd, and redirect its output to ~/cmd.txt:
`$ echo cmd > ~/cmd.txt`

2. To verify that the file contains the correct output, you can use the cat command:
`$ cat ~/cmd.txt`
This command should output cmd, confirming that the echo command's output was correctly redirected to the file.

Question 34: Network File System (NFS) Configuration and Automatic Mounting

On a Linux server named Node1, which is configured as an NFS client, your task is to configure the system to automatically mount the NFS share located at Node2:/share on the /nfs directory at boot time. Ensure that the NFS services are running on both Node1 and Node2. Also, verify that the NFS share is successfully mounted on Node1 by listing the contents of the /nfs directory.

Explanation

1. Install NFS Client: Depending on your Linux distribution, the command to install NFS client may vary.

For Ubuntu, you can use:
```
$ sudo apt-get install nfs-common
```

For CentOS, you can use:
```
$ sudo yum install nfs-utils
```

2. Create Mount Point: Create the /nfs directory using:
```
$ sudo mkdir /nfs
```

3. Edit /etc/fstab File: Open the /etc/fstab file in a text editor with root privileges.

Add the following line to the end of the file:
```
Node2:/share /nfs nfs defaults 0 0
```
This line tells the system to mount the NFS share located at Node2:/share on the /nfs directory at boot time.

4. Mount NFS Share: Use the command:
`$ sudo mount -a`
to mount the NFS share. The -a option tells the system to mount all filesystems mentioned in /etc/fstab.

5. Verify Mount: Verify that the NFS share is successfully mounted by using:
`$ ls /nfs`

Question 35: Creating a Docker Image with Containerfile for Web Server Deployment

Your task involves configuring a Linux server named Node1 to create a Docker image named "hello_world". This image should be based on the Red Hat Universal Base Image 8 Init (ubi8/ubi-init) and should include a web server (httpd) configured to start automatically via systemd when the container is running. The web server should display "Hello World!" when accessed and be exposed on port 80. After creating the Containerfile, build the "hello_world" image and run a new container from this image, naming it "hello_world_run".

Explanation

To accomplish the task of creating a Docker image with a Containerfile for web server deployment on Node1 in a distribution-agnostic approach, follow these steps:

1. Create Containerfile: Begin by creating a Containerfile named Containerfile in a directory of your choice. This file will contain instructions for building the Docker image. Open a text editor and add the following content to Containerfile:

```
FROM ubi8/ubi-init

# Install httpd package
RUN yum install -y httpd

# Configure httpd to start automatically via systemd
RUN systemctl enable httpd

# Set up web server content
```

```
RUN echo "Hello World!" > /var/www/html/index.html

# Expose port 80
EXPOSE 80

# Start systemd service as the container's entry point
CMD ["/sbin/init"]
```

This Containerfile specifies that the Docker image should be based on the Red Hat Universal Base Image 8 Init (ubi8/ubi-init). It installs the httpd package, configures it to start automatically via systemd, sets up a simple "Hello World!" web page, exposes port 80, and sets /sbin/init as the container's entry point.

2. Build Docker Image: After creating the Containerfile, navigate to the directory containing it and build the Docker image named "hello_world". Use the following command:
```
$ docker build -t hello_world .
```
This command builds the Docker image using the instructions specified in the Containerfile (. indicates the current directory).

3. Run Container: Once the Docker image is built, you can run a new container from this image, naming it "hello_world_run". Use the following command:
```
$ docker run -d --name hello_world_run -p 80:80 hello_world
```
This command creates a new container named "hello_world_run" from the "hello_world" image, runs it in detached mode (-d), and maps port 80 of the host to port 80 of the container (-p 80:80).

4. Verify Container: To ensure that the container is running and the web server is accessible, you can check the status of the container:
```
$ docker ps
```

This command lists all running containers. You should see the "hello_world_run" container in the list.

5. Access Web Server: Finally, you can access the web server from a web browser or using curl. Open a web browser and navigate to http://<Node1_IP> or use curl:

```
$ curl http://<Node1_IP>
```

Replace <Node1_IP> with the IP address of Node1. You should see the "Hello World!" message displayed, indicating that the web server is functioning correctly.

Question 36: User Account Management and File System Permissions

As a system administrator, you are tasked with ensuring that every new user account created on your Linux system has a file named "Note" in their home directory. This file should be automatically created upon account creation. The file should have read and write permissions for the user, but no permissions for the group and others.

Explanation

To solve this task, we can leverage the /etc/skel directory. Files and directories placed in /etc/skel will be copied into a new user's home directory when the user is created with the useradd command.

Here are the steps to accomplish this:

1. Create a file named "Note" in the /etc/skel directory. You can use the touch command to create an empty file:
$ sudo touch /etc/skel/Note

2. Set the appropriate permissions for the "Note" file. We want the user to have read and write permissions, but no permissions for the group and others. We can use the chmod command to accomplish this:
$ sudo chmod 600 /etc/skel/Note
Now, every time a new user is created, they will have a file named "Note" in their home directory with the appropriate permissions.

Explanation:

- The /etc/skel directory in Linux is used as a template for new user's home directories. When a new user is created with the useradd command, files and directories from /etc/skel are copied into the new user's home directory.
- The touch command is used to create a new empty file.
- The chmod command is used to change the permissions of a file or directory. In this case, we used chmod 600, which sets read and write permissions for the user, but no permissions for the group and others (6 corresponds to read and write permissions, and 0 corresponds to no permissions).

LFCS PRACTICE EXAM THREE

Question 1: Archives and Compression

As a system administrator, you're tasked with the following:

1. Archive Creation and Compression: Create a tar archive of the directory /var/log, compress it using the gzip algorithm, and move the compressed file to the /backups directory.
2. Archive Extraction: Extract the compressed tar archive in the /backups directory to a new directory /restored_logs.
3. File Size: Determine the size of the compressed file in the /backups directory.

Explanation

1. Archive Creation and Compression:
```
$ sudo tar -czvf /var/log.tar.gz /var/log
$ sudo mv /var/log.tar.gz /backups/
```

2. Archive Extraction:

To extract the compressed tar archive located in the /backups directory to a new directory /restored_logs, use the following command:
```
$ sudo mkdir /restored_logs
$ sudo tar -xzvf /backups/log.tar.gz -C /restored_logs
```

3. File Size:

To determine the size of the compressed file in the /backups directory, utilize the du command:
```
$ du -sh /backups/log.tar.gz
```

Question 2: File Operations

As a system administrator, you're tasked with the following:

1. Find and List Files: Identify and list all files in the /opt directory that have not been accessed or modified in the last 7 days.
2. File Size: Determine the size of each file that meets the criteria of not being accessed or modified in the last 7 days in the /opt directory.
3. File Permissions: Display the permissions of each file that has not been accessed or modified in the last 7 days in the /opt directory.

Explanation

1. Find and List Files:

To find and list all files in the /opt directory that have not been accessed or modified in the last 7 days, use the following command:
```
$ sudo find /opt -type f -not -atime -7 -not -mtime -7 -ls
```

2. File Size:

To determine the size of each file that meets the criteria of not being accessed or modified in the last 7 days in the /opt directory, employ the find command with the -exec option and the du command:
```
$ sudo find /opt -type f -not -atime -7 -not -mtime -7 -exec du -sh {} \;
```

3. File Permissions:

To display the permissions of each file that has not been accessed or modified in the last 7 days in the /opt directory, utilize the find command with the -exec option and the ls command:

```
$ sudo find /opt -type f -not -atime -7 -not -mtime -7 -exec ls -l {} \;
```

Question 3: Network Configuration and DNS Setup

As a system administrator, you've been assigned the following network configuration duties:

1. Dynamic IP Address Assignment: Configure a dynamic IP address for the network interface eth1 using DHCP. Ensure proper hostname resolution using DNS.
2. Network Interface Status: Verify the status of the network interface eth1.
3. DNS Configuration: Configure the system to utilize Google's DNS servers (8.8.8.8 and 8.8.4.4) for hostname resolution.

Explanation

1. Dynamic IP Address Assignment: To configure a dynamic IP address for the network interface eth1 using DHCP, you'll typically use a network configuration tool such as systemd-networkd, NetworkManager, or ifupdown. Here's how you can do it using ifupdown:

```
$ sudo nano /etc/network/interfaces
```

Add the following lines to the file:

```
auto eth1
iface eth1 inet dhcp
```

Save the file and exit the text editor. Then, apply the changes:

```
$ sudo ifdown eth1 && sudo ifup eth1
```

This will bring down and then bring up the eth1 interface, allowing it to obtain an IP address dynamically from a DHCP server on the network.

2. Network Interface Status: To verify the status of the

network interface eth1, you can use the ip command:

```
$ ip addr show eth1
```

This command will display information about the eth1 interface, including its IP address, subnet mask, and other relevant details.

3. DNS Configuration: To configure the system to utilize Google's DNS servers (8.8.8.8 and 8.8.4.4) for hostname resolution, you need to edit the /etc/resolv.conf file:

```
$ sudo nano /etc/resolv.conf
```

Add the following lines to the file:

```
nameserver 8.8.8.8
nameserver 8.8.4.4
```

Save the file and exit the text editor. These lines specify Google's DNS servers as the nameservers for hostname resolution.

4. Verify DNS Configuration: To verify that the system is using the configured DNS servers for hostname resolution, you can use the nslookup or dig command:

```
$ nslookup example.com
```

or

```
$ dig example.com
```

Replace example.com with the domain you want to look up. The output should display information retrieved from Google's DNS servers if the configuration is successful.

Question 4: Advanced Docker Container Configuration and Management

As a system administrator, you are tasked with the following duties:

1. Installing Docker: Install Docker on a Linux system. Ensure that the Docker service is enabled and running.

2. Creating a Dockerfile: Create a Dockerfile for a Python web application. The application should be built using Flask and should return "Hello, World!" when accessed.

3. Building a Docker Image: Use the Dockerfile to build a Docker image.

4. Running a Docker Container: Run a Docker container from the image you built. The container should restart automatically if it stops.

5. Exposing the Application: Expose the Python web application running in the Docker container on port 8000 of the host machine.

6. Testing the Application: Use curl or a web browser to test that the application is running and accessible.

Explanation

1. Installing Docker: You can install Docker on a Linux system using the package manager for your specific distribution. For example, on Ubuntu, you would use apt:

```
$ sudo apt update
$ sudo apt install docker.io
$ sudo systemctl start docker
$ sudo systemctl enable docker
```

2. Creating a Dockerfile: Here's a simple Dockerfile for a Python

Flask application:

```
FROM python:3.7
WORKDIR /app
COPY . /app
RUN pip install flask
EXPOSE 5000
CMD ["python", "app.py"]
```

In this Dockerfile, we're using the official Python 3.7 image from Docker Hub as our base image. We then copy our application into the /app directory in the container, install Flask using pip, expose port 5000 (the default port for Flask), and finally, specify that the container should run app.py when it starts.

3. Building a Docker Image: You can build a Docker image from the Dockerfile using the docker build command:

```
$ docker build -t my-python-app .
```

4. Running a Docker Container: You can run a Docker container from the image using the docker run command:

```
$ docker run -d --restart=always -p 8000:5000 my-python-app
```

5. Exposing the Application: In the docker run command above, the -p 8000:5000 option maps port 8000 on the host to port 5000 in the container, effectively exposing the Flask application on port 8000 of the host machine.

6. Testing the Application: You can test the application using curl:

```
$ curl http://localhost:8000
```

You should see "Hello, World!" in the response if everything is working correctly. If you have a web browser installed on the system, you can also navigate to http://localhost:8000 to test the application.

Question 5: Text Manipulation

As a system administrator, you're required to do the following tasks:

Tasks:

1. Text Extraction: Extract lines 15 to 25 from a file named '~/mytext' and save them to a new file named "~/section.txt".
2. Search and Replace: Find all occurrences of the word "error" in the '~/mytext' file and replace them with "warning".
3. Word Count: Determine the total number of words in the '~/mytext' file and display the result.
4. Appending Lines: Add the text "This is the end" to the end of the '~/mytext' file.
5. Line Count: Determine the total number of lines in the '~/mytext' file and display the result.
6. File Permissions: Change the permissions of the '~/mytext' file to read and write for the owner, and read-only for the group and others.

Assuming the Content of 'mytext' is as follows:

1. Introduction to Linux
2. Basic Commands and Navigation
3. File Systems and Permissions
4. Shell Scripting
5. Error Handling and Logging
6. Networking Essentials
7. System Administration Tasks
8. Security Best Practices
9. Package Management
10. Troubleshooting Techniques
11. Advanced Networking Configurations

12. Docker and Containerization
13. Cloud Computing Basics
14. Kernel and Process Management
15. System Recovery Procedures

This is a sample text file for LFCS practice.

Explanation

1. Text Extraction: To extract lines 15 to 25 from a file named 'mytext' and save them to a new file named "section.txt", you can use the sed command:
```
$ sed -n '15,25p' mytext > ~/section.txt
```

2. Search and Replace: To find all occurrences of the word "error" in the 'mytext' file and replace them with "warning", you can use sed with the -i option for in-place editing:
```
$ sed -i 's/error/warning/g' mytext
```

3. Word Count: To determine the total number of words in the 'mytext' file and display the result, you can use the wc command with the -w option:
```
$ wc -w mytext
```

4. Appending Lines: To add the text "This is the end" to the end of the 'mytext' file, you can use the echo command with output redirection:
```
$ echo "This is the end" >> mytext
```

5. Line Count: To determine the total number of lines in the 'mytext' file and display the result, you can use the wc command with the -l option:
```
$ wc -l mytext
```

6. File Permissions: To change the permissions of the 'mytext' file to read and write for the owner, and read-only for the

group and others, you can use the chmod command:

```
$ chmod 644 mytext
```

Question 6: Bash Scripting

As a system administrator, you're tasked with writing a Bash script "~/script.sh" that performs the following tasks:

1. Displays the value of the PATH environment variable.
2. Accepts a filename as a command-line argument, verifies if the file exists and is writable, and outputs an appropriate message.
3. Defines a function to calculate the square of a given number.
4. Accepts two numbers as command-line arguments and prints their sum.

Explanation

```bash
#!/bin/bash

# Ask the user to enter a filename
read -p "Enter a filename: " filename

# Display the value of the PATH environment variable
echo "PATH: $PATH"

# Check if the entered filename exists and is writable
if [[ -w "$filename" ]]; then
    echo "The file '$filename' exists and is writable."
else
    echo "The file '$filename' does not exist or is not writable."
fi

# Define a function to calculate the square of a number
function square {
  local num=$1
  echo $((num*num))
```

```
}

# Accept two numbers as command-line arguments and print
their sum
read -p "Enter the first number: " num1
read -p "Enter the second number: " num2
echo "The sum of $num1 and $num2 is: $((num1+num2))"

# Calculate the square of a number
echo "The square of $num1 is: $(square $num1)"
echo "The square of $num2 is: $(square $num2)"
```

Save the script to a file "script.sh".

Make the script executable with the command:
$ chmod +x ~/script.sh

Run the script with the command:
$ ./script.sh

Question 7: Package Management

As a system administrator, you need to install the htop package.

Explanation

1. Using APT (Debian/Ubuntu): APT (Advanced Package Tool) is the package manager used in Debian-based distributions such as Debian and Ubuntu. Use the following command to install the htop package:
```
$ sudo apt update
$ sudo apt install htop
```

 # apt update: Updates the local package index to ensure you have the latest information about available packages.
 # apt install htop: Installs the htop package.

2. Using YUM (CentOS/RHEL 7 and earlier): YUM (Yellowdog Updater, Modified) is the package manager used in CentOS, RHEL, and other Red Hat-based distributions. Use the following command to install the htop package:
```
$ sudo yum install epel-release   # Install EPEL repository (for CentOS/RHEL)
$ sudo yum update
$ sudo yum install htop
```

 # yum install epel-release: Installs the EPEL (Extra Packages for Enterprise Linux) repository, which contains additional packages not included in the default repositories.
 # yum update: Updates the local package index.
 # yum install htop: Installs the htop package.

3. Using DNF (CentOS/RHEL 8 and later): DNF (Dandified YUM)

is the next-generation package manager used in CentOS/RHEL 8 and later versions. Use the following command to install the htop package:

`$ sudo dnf install htop`

This command installs the htop package.

4. Verification: After installing the htop package, you can verify its installation by running the htop command:

`$ htop`

This command launches the htop utility, a dynamic real-time process viewer.

Question 8: Cron Job Management

As a system administrator, you need to schedule a cron job to execute a script named ~/daily_backup.sh at midnight every day. This script backs up the /etc directory.

Explanation

1. Open the Crontab File:

Use the crontab -e command to open the crontab file for editing. If this is your first time running this command, it may prompt you to select an editor. You can choose nano for a simple interface.

2. Add the Cron Job:

In the crontab file, add the following line to schedule the ~/ daily_backup.sh script to run at midnight every day:
`0 0 * * * /path/to/daily_backup.sh`
This line instructs cron to run the script at minute 0 of hour 0 of every day of the month, every month, and every day of the week.

3. Save and Close the Crontab File:

If you're using nano, press Ctrl+O to save the file, then Ctrl+X to exit. If you're using vi, press Esc, then type :wq and press Enter.

4. Verify the Cron Job:

Use the crontab -l command to list your current cron jobs and verify that the new job has been added.

Question 9: User and Group Management with Password Policy Enforcement

As a system administrator, you're required to perform the following tasks:

1. Create a New Group: Create a new group named "finance".
2. Add a New User to the Group: Add a new user named "accountant" to the "finance" group.
3. Modify Password Policy: Modify the password policy to enforce a minimum length of 8 characters and require at least one special character.

Explanation

1. Create a New Group: Use the groupadd command to create a new group named "finance":
$ sudo groupadd finance
This command creates a new group named "finance" on the system.

2. Add a New User to the Group: Use the useradd command to add a new user named "accountant" and specify the primary group as "finance":
$ sudo useradd -m -G finance accountant
-m: Creates the user's home directory if it doesn't exist.
-G: Specifies additional groups to which the user belongs. In this case, "finance" is specified as the primary group.

3. Modify Password Policy: Password policy enforcement can vary depending on the Linux distribution and the tools available. Here's how to enforce a minimum length of 8 characters and require at least one special character using

common tools:

- Using PAM (Pluggable Authentication Modules): PAM provides a flexible mechanism for enforcing password policies. Edit the /etc/pam.d/common-password file and add the following line:
`password requisite pam_cracklib.so minlen=8 ucredit=-1`
This line specifies that passwords must have a minimum length of 8 characters (minlen=8) and must contain at least one uppercase character (ucredit=-1).

- Using passwd command: Some distributions offer the passwd command with options to set password complexity rules. For example, on systems using passwd, you can set a minimum password length and require at least one special character by executing:
`$ sudo passwd --minlength=8 --stdin --mindiff=3 accountant`
This command sets the minimum password length to 8 characters and requires at least one special character.

4. Test Password Policy Enforcement: To verify that the password policy is enforced, try changing the password for the "accountant" user:
`$ sudo passwd accountant`
Follow the prompts to enter a new password. If the password does not meet the specified criteria, you'll receive an error message indicating the policy violation.

Question 10: Customizing the Message of the Day (MOTD) to Display Critical System Resource Information

Perform the following tasks to configure a custom system-wide Message of the Day (MOTD) that displays critical system resource information and ensure it appears upon user login:

1. Display System Time and Date: Configure the MOTD to display the current system time and date.
2. Present System Uptime: Include information about the system uptime in the MOTD.
3. List Total Number of Users Logged In: Showcase the total number of users currently logged in.
4. Showcase System Load Averages: Display the system load averages for the past 1, 5, and 15 minutes.
5. Verify your configuration by logging into the system.

Explanation

1. Create a Custom MOTD Script: Create a custom MOTD script to gather system resource information and display it to users upon login. Create a new file, for example, /etc/update-motd.d/99-custom-motd, and make it executable:

```
$ sudo touch /etc/update-motd.d/99-custom-motd
$ sudo chmod +x /etc/update-motd.d/99-custom-motd
```

Edit the file using a text editor:

```
$ sudo nano /etc/update-motd.d/99-custom-motd
```

Add the following content to the file:

```
#!/bin/bash
```

```
# Display system time and date
echo "Current Time and Date: $(date)"

# Present system uptime
echo "System Uptime: $(uptime -p)"

# List total number of users logged in
echo "Total Users Logged In: $(who | wc -l)"

# Showcase system load averages
echo "System Load Averages (1m, 5m, 15m): $(cat /proc/
loadavg | awk '{print $1 "," $2 "," $3}')"
```

Save and close the file (Ctrl + X, then Y, then Enter).

2. Verify Configuration: To verify that the custom MOTD script is working correctly, you can manually execute it:
$ sudo /etc/update-motd.d/99-custom-motd

This command should display the system resource information as defined in the script.

3. Test the MOTD upon User Login: Log out of the system and log back in to verify that the custom MOTD is displayed upon user login. The MOTD should automatically appear before the command prompt after successful login.

Question 11: System Monitoring, Logging, and User Management

Perform the following tasks:

1. Configure System Logging: Configure system logging to capture kernel messages. `/var/log/kernel.log` is the log file where these messages should be stored.
2. View System Logs: Demonstrate how to view these logs for critical system events.
3. User Account Management: Disable the user account "tempadmin". Ensure that all active sessions for this user are terminated immediately.
4. Verify User Account Status: Verify that "tempadmin" cannot log in by attempting to log in as this user.

Explanation

1. Configure System Logging: To capture kernel messages, edit the syslog configuration file. The location of this file may vary slightly depending on the distribution. For most systems, it is located at /etc/syslog.conf or /etc/rsyslog.conf. Add the following line to the configuration file to capture kernel messages:

kern.* /var/log/kernel.log

This line instructs the system to log all kernel messages to the file /var/log/kernel.log.

2. View System Logs: After configuring logging, you can view system logs using the tail, grep, or less commands. For example, to view the last 20 lines of the kernel log file:

$ tail -n 20 /var/log/kernel.log

An example of a critical system event in the logs could be an out-of-memory (OOM) error. This error indicates that the system has run out of memory and may result in instability or crashing of applications. To interpret an OOM event, look for lines containing "Out of memory" or "OOM" in the kernel log file. These lines typically include information about the process that triggered the OOM event and may provide insights into the cause of the memory exhaustion.

3. User Account Management: To disable the user account "tempadmin" and terminate all active sessions, you can use the usermod command with the -L flag to lock the account:
```
$ sudo usermod -L tempadmin
```

This command disables the account by locking the password, preventing any further logins.

4. Verify User Account Status: To verify that the "tempadmin" user cannot log in, attempt to log in as this user:
```
$ su - tempadmin
```

If the account is successfully disabled, you should receive a message indicating that the account is locked or disabled.

Question 12: Networking and File Systems

1. Identify and display information about the active network connections on the system. Include the following details in your output:

- *Protocol type*
- *Local and foreign addresses*
- *Connection state*

2. Create a new partition /dev/sdc1 with a size of 200MB. Format it with the ext3 filesystem. Provide the command to verify the filesystem type of the new partition.

3. Mount the new partition at /mnt/data, and ensure it gets mounted automatically at boot.

Explanation

1. Display active network connections:
$ sudo netstat -tunapl

2. Create a new partition and format it:
$ sudo parted /dev/sdc mkpart primary ext3 1MiB 200MiB
$ sudo mkfs.ext3 /dev/sdc1
$ sudo blkid /dev/sdc1

3. Mount the new partition:
$ echo '/dev/sdc1 /mnt/data ext3 defaults 0 0' | sudo tee -a /etc/fstab
$ sudo mkdir /mnt/data
$ sudo mount -a
$ df -hT | grep /mnt/data

Explanation:

- The netstat command is used to display active network connections, including details like protocol type, local and foreign addresses, and connection state.
- For creating the new partition and formatting it, the parted and mkfs.ext3 commands are utilized. The blkid command helps verify the filesystem type of the new partition.
- To ensure the new partition gets mounted automatically at boot, the fstab file is updated accordingly. The mount command is then used to mount the partition at /mnt/data, and df -hT is employed to confirm its successful mounting.

Question 13: Privilege Management

You are the system administrator for a server running MySQL. A new team member, "manager2", needs the ability to restart the MySQL service in case of issues. However, it's crucial to follow security best practices and grant minimal privileges.

Task: Configure the system to allow "manager2" to restart the MySQL service using sudo without a password prompt. Focus on achieving this with the principle of least privilege in mind.

Explanation

1. Create User with Restricted Shell (Security Measure):
$ sudo useradd -M manager2

This command creates the user "manager2" with the -M option, assigning a restricted shell for enhanced security.

2. Secure Password Management:
Enforce strong password practices for "manager2".

3. Grant sudo Access for Specific Command (Least Privilege):

Option A: Using sudoers file (Recommended):
$ echo 'manager2 ALL=(root) NOPASSWD: /usr/sbin/systemctl restart mysql.service' | sudo tee /etc/sudoers.d/manager2

Option B: Using visudo (Alternative):

Editing the sudoers file directly can lead to security issues if done incorrectly. It's recommended to use the visudo command.

```
$ sudo visudo
```

Add the following line:
```
manager2 ALL=(root) NOPASSWD: /usr/sbin/systemctl restart
mysql.service
```

Save the changes and exit.

4. Verification:
```
$ su - manager2 -c 'sudo /usr/sbin/systemctl restart
mysql.service'
```

If successful, the service restarts without a password prompt.

Question 14: Storage Management

The logical volume named "mylv" within the volume group "myvg" is running low on space. You need to increase its size by 100MB.

Task: Expand the logical volume "mylv" in the volume group "myvg" by 100MB. Verify the size of the logical volume before and after the operation. If there's insufficient free space in the volume group, outline the steps to add a new physical volume for further expansion.

Explanation

1. Increase the size of the logical volume named mylv in the volume group myvg by 100MB.

# Check the current size of the logical volume
$ sudo lvdisplay /dev/myvg/mylv

# Increase the size of the logical volume by 100MB
$ sudo lvextend -L +100M /dev/myvg/mylv

-L: specifies the size to extend the logical volume by. Here, "+100M" indicates an increase of 100 Megabytes.
/dev/myvg/mylv: specifies the path to the logical volume to be extended.

# Resize the filesystem to fit the new size of the logical volume
$ sudo resize2fs /dev/myvg/mylv

# Verify the new size of the logical volume
$ sudo lvdisplay /dev/myvg/mylv

2. If there is not enough free space in the volume group, follow these steps to add a new physical volume:

Assuming /dev/sdb is the new disk you want to add

# Create a new physical volume
$ sudo pvcreate /dev/sdb

# Extend the volume group
$ sudo vgextend myvg /dev/sdb

# Now you can retry increasing the size of the logical volume
$ sudo lvextend -L +100M /dev/myvg/mylv
$ sudo resize2fs /dev/myvg/mylv

Question 15: System Logging and Text Processing

You have a system log file (/var/log/messages) containing various system events.

Tasks:

1. Filter Specific Messages: Find all lines in the file that begin with the word "core".
2. Save Filtered Output: Redirect the filtered lines to a new file (/opt/core_logs.txt). If the file already exists, append the new results instead of overwriting it.

Explanation

1. Filtering and Saving:
```
$ grep '^core' /var/log/messages >> /opt/core_logs.txt
```

grep '^core' /var/log/messages: Filters lines in /var/log/ messages that start with "core" (using the ^ symbol for beginning-of-line match).
>> /opt/core_logs.txt: Appends the filtered output to /opt/ core_logs.txt.

Verification:
```
$ cat /opt/core_logs.txt | head -n 10
```
View the first 10 lines (optional)

cat /opt/core_logs.txt: Displays the content of the log file.
head -n 10: Limits output to the first 10 lines (optional, for quick verification).

Question 16: File Comparison and Directory Analysis

You have two files (test1 and test2) and two directories (dir1 and dir2) in your home directory.

Tasks:

1. Find Unique Line: Identify a single line present in only one of the files (test1 or test2). Capture this unique line and save it to a file (/opt/difference.txt).
2. Identify Missing Files: Find files existing in dir1 but not in dir2. Append a list of these missing files to the same file (/opt/difference.txt). Existing content in /opt/difference.txt should be preserved (append the result).

Explanation

1. Finding Unique Line:
```
$ comm -12 ~/test1 ~/test2 >> /opt/difference.txt
```

comm -12 ~/test1 ~/test2: Uses the comm command to compare files line by line.
-1: Shows lines only present in the first file (test1).
-2: Shows lines only present in the second file (test2).
~/test1 ~/test2: Specifies the files to be compared.
>> /opt/difference.txt: Appends the unique line(s) to the specified file.

2. Identifying Missing Files:
```
$ comm -d ~/dir1/ ~/dir2/ >> /opt/difference.txt
```

comm -d ~/dir1/ ~/dir2/: Uses the comm command to compare directory listings.

 # -d: Shows only entries present in the first file (dir1) but not in the second (dir2).

 # ~/dir1/ ~/dir2/: Specifies the directories to be compared (using directory listing as input).

 # >> /opt/difference.txt: Appends the list of missing files to the specified file.

Question 17: File Permissions and Attributes

You manage files in your home directory.

Tasks:

1. Grant Read Access (confidential.docx): The file "confidential.docx" currently only allows "jane" to read it. Add read access for "john" while preserving other permissions.
2. Remove Immutable Attribute (archive.tar.gz): The file "archive.tar.gz" has the immutable attribute set, preventing modifications. Remove this attribute to allow changes.

Explanation

1. Modifying ACL (confidential.docx):
`$ sudo setfacl -m u:john:r ~/confidential.docx`

sudo: Required for administrative tasks (modifying ACLs).
setfacl: Manages file Access Control Lists (ACLs).
-m: Modifies existing ACL entries.
u:john:r: Adds a new entry for user "john" with read ("r") permission only.
~/confidential.docx: Specifies the file to modify.

2. Removing Immutable Attribute (archive.tar.gz):
`$ sudo chattr -i ~/archive.tar.gz`

sudo: Required for administrative tasks (changing file attributes).
chattr: Changes file attributes.
-i: Removes the immutable attribute.
~/archive.tar.gz: Specifies the file to modify.

Verification:

- Use getfacl ~/confidential.docx to verify the updated ACL entries.

- Use lsattr ~/archive.tar.gz to confirm the removal of the immutable attribute.

Question 18: Process Management and Signals

Task: On your Linux system, a process named httpd is currently running. Your objective is to send the SIGHUP signal to this process. The SIGHUP signal is commonly utilized to prompt a process to reload its configuration files. It's crucial to ensure that only the httpd process is affected, without impacting any other running processes.

Explanation

1. Send the SIGHUP signal:

The httpd process is typically associated with the Apache HTTP server. To dispatch the SIGHUP signal to the httpd process, you can employ either the pkill or killall command:

`$ sudo pkill -HUP httpd`
or
`$ sudo killall -HUP httpd`

Explanation: Both the pkill and killall commands target processes by name. The -HUP option designates the SIGHUP signal, while httpd specifies the name of the process.

Verify the status of the httpd process using ps or top to confirm the operation's success. For instance:
`$ ps aux | grep httpd`

This command presents the status of the httpd process. Following a successful operation, you should observe the httpd process running with a new process ID (PID) because the SIGHUP signal triggers the process to restart. If the httpd process fails to restart, inspect the system logs for any error messages.

Question 19: Network Configuration and Packet Forwarding

On a Linux server named Node1, your task is to enable packet forwarding for IPV4. This involves modifying the system's network configuration to allow it to forward network packets from one network interface to another.

Explanation

1. Open the /etc/sysctl.conf file in a text editor. You might use vi, nano, or another text editor, depending on your preference:
$ sudo vi /etc/sysctl.conf

2. Add the following line to the end of the file:
net.ipv4.ip_forward = 1
This line enables packet forwarding for IPV4.

3. Save and close the file.

4. Apply the changes with the sysctl command:
$ sudo sysctl -p

5. To verify that packet forwarding has been correctly enabled, you can use the sysctl command with the net.ipv4.ip_forward parameter:
sysctl net.ipv4.ip_forward
This command should return net.ipv4.ip_forward = 1, confirming that packet forwarding for IPV4 is enabled.

Question 20: Network Configuration and IPV6 Packet Forwarding

On a Linux server named Node1, your task is to enable IPV6 packet forwarding. This involves modifying the system's network configuration to allow it to forward network packets from one network interface to another. This configuration should persist even after the system is rebooted.

Explanation

1. Open the /etc/sysctl.conf file in a text editor. You might use vi, nano, or another text editor, depending on your preference:
`$ sudo vi /etc/sysctl.conf`

2. Add the following line to the end of the file:
`net.ipv6.conf.all.forwarding = 1`
This line enables packet forwarding for IPV6.

3. Save and close the file.

4. Apply the changes with the sysctl command:
`$ sudo sysctl -p`

5. To verify that IPV6 packet forwarding has been correctly enabled, you can use the sysctl command with the net.ipv6.conf.all.forwarding parameter:
`$ sysctl net.ipv6.conf.all.forwarding`

This command should return net.ipv6.conf.all.forwarding = 1, confirming that IPV6 packet forwarding is enabled.

Question 21: System Scheduling and Automation

As a system administrator, you are required to schedule a task that will help remind your team to take regular breaks for their health and productivity.

You need to schedule a cron job that prints the message "Break Time!" every two hours on weekdays (Monday to Friday). The message should be displayed on the current terminal screen of all logged-in users. The cron job should be performed by the root user.

Explanation

To accomplish this task, we need to edit the root user's crontab. Here's how you can do it:
$ sudo crontab -e

This command will open the root user's crontab file in the default text editor. Add the following line to schedule the task:
0 */2 * * 1-5 echo "Break Time!" | wall

Here's what each field means in the cron syntax:
0 represents the minute of the hour when the task should run. In this case, it's at the start of the hour.
**/2* means the task should run every two hours.
The first * is for the day of the month, and we want it to run every day, so we leave it as *.
The second * is for the month, and we want it to run every month, so we leave it as *.
1-5 represents the days of the week, from Monday (1) to Friday (5).
The *echo "Break Time!" | wall* command sends the message

"Break Time!" to all logged-in users.

To check if the cron job has been set up correctly, you can list the current user's cron jobs with the following command:
`$ sudo crontab -l`

This command will list all the cron jobs set up by the root user. You should see the cron job you just added in the output. If you see the cron job, it means it has been set up correctly. If not, you may need to revisit the steps above.

Question 22: Disk Partitioning and File System Management

As a system administrator, you are required to manage disk storage on a server. Your task is to create a new partition on the /dev/sde disk. The partition should have the following specifications:

1. The size of the partition should be 512MB.
2. The partition should be formatted with an ext4 file system.
3. The partition should be automatically mounted at startup under the /mnt/data directory.

Explanation

1. Create a new partition: First, you need to create a new partition on /dev/sde. You can use the fdisk utility for this. The command sudo fdisk /dev/sde will open the utility. Once inside, you can press n to create a new partition, choose the defaults for the partition number and the first sector, and for the last sector, type +512M to create a 512MB partition. Then, press w to write the changes.

```
$ sudo fdisk /dev/sde
> n
> p
> 1
>
> +512M
> w
```

2. Format the new partition: After creating the partition (let's assume it's /dev/sde1), you need to format it with the ext4 file system. You can use the mkfs.ext4 command for this.

```
$ sudo mkfs.ext4 /dev/sde1
```

3. Mount the partition: Before you can use the partition, you need to mount it. First, create a mount point with mkdir, then use mount to mount the partition.

```
$ sudo mkdir /mnt/data
$ sudo mount /dev/sde1 /mnt/data
```

4. Automatically mount at startup: To ensure the partition is mounted automatically at startup, you need to add an entry to the /etc/fstab file. You can use echo and tee to do this. The entry should look like this: /dev/sde1 /mnt/data ext4 defaults 0 0.

```
$ echo '/dev/sde1 /mnt/data ext4 defaults 0 0' | sudo tee -a /etc/fstab
```

Question 23: User Management
and Shell Configuration

As a system administrator, you are tasked with managing user accounts on a Linux server. One of the users, sam, has requested to change his default login shell to zsh. Your task is to:

1. Verify if zsh is installed on the system. If not, install it.
2. Change sam's default login shell to zsh.
3. Ensure that the change does not affect other users.
4. Verify that the change has been successfully applied.

Explanation

1. Check if zsh is installed: You can use the which command to check if zsh is installed. If zsh is installed, this command will return the path to the zsh executable.
```
$ which zsh
```
If zsh is not installed, you will need to install it. The command to install zsh depends on your package manager. On Debian-based systems, you would use apt-get, and on Red Hat-based systems, you would use yum or dnf.

```
# Debian-based systems
$ sudo apt-get install zsh
```

```
# Red Hat-based systems
$ sudo yum install zsh
```
2. Change the user's login shell: You can use the chsh command to change the user's login shell. The -s option is used to specify the shell, and you should replace /bin/zsh with the path returned by which zsh.
```
$ sudo chsh -s /bin/zsh sam
```

3. Verify the change: You can verify the change by checking the user's entry in the passwd file in the /etc/ directory. The shell is listed as the last field in the user's entry.

`$ grep sam /etc/passwd`

Question 24: User Management and Account Expiration

As a system administrator, you are tasked with managing user accounts on a Linux server. Your task is to:

1. Create a new user named john.
2. The user should have a User ID (UID) of 1250.
3. The account should expire on December 21, 2027.

Explanation

1. Create a new user with a specific UID: You can use the useradd command to create a new user. The -u option is used to specify the UID.
```
$ sudo useradd -u 1250 john
```

2. Set the account expiration date: You can use the chage command to set the account expiration date. The -E option is used to specify the expiration date in the format YYYY-MM-DD.
```
$ sudo chage -E 2027-12-21 john
```

3. Verify the changes: You can verify the changes by checking the user's entry in the passwd and shadow files. The UID is the third field in the user's entry in the passwd file, and the expiration date is the eighth field in the user's entry in the shadow file.
```
$ grep john /etc/passwd
$ grep john /etc/shadow
```

Question 25: File Permissions and Ownership

As a system administrator, you are tasked with managing files and permissions on a Linux server. Your task is to:

1. Copy the hosts file in the /etc directory to the /var/ directory and rename it to "nhosts".
2. Change the permissions of the "nhosts" file such that:
3. User "sam" can read, write, and execute the file.
4. User "john" can only read the file.

Explanation

1. Copy the file: You can use the cp command to copy the hosts file to the /var/ directory and rename it to "nhosts".
$ sudo cp /etc/hosts /var/nhosts

2. Change the file ownership: You can use the chown command to change the owner of the "nhosts" file to "sam".
$ sudo chown sam /var/nhosts

3. Set the file permissions: You can use the chmod command to set the permissions of the "nhosts" file. The permissions should be set such that "sam" can read (4), write (2), and execute (1) the file (sum is 7), and "john" can only read the file (4).
$ sudo chmod 740 /var/nhosts

Question 26: Logical Volume Management and Filesystem Expansion

As a system administrator, you are tasked with managing storage on a Linux server. Your task is to:

1. Create a 4GiB LVM volume group named "vgroup" using the /dev/sdf disk.
2. Inside the "vgroup" LVM volume group, create a 1GiB LVM logical volume named "lvol".
3. Format the "lvol" LVM logical volume with the ext4 filesystem.
4. Mount the "lvol" LVM logical volume persistently on the "/lvol" directory.
5. Extend the ext4 filesystem on "lvol" by 100M.

Explanation

1. Create a physical volume: You can use the pvcreate command to create a physical volume on /dev/sdf.
$ sudo pvcreate /dev/sdf

2. Create a volume group: You can use the vgcreate command to create a volume group named "vgroup" on the physical volume /dev/sdf.
$ sudo vgcreate vgroup /dev/sdf

3. Create a logical volume: You can use the lvcreate command to create a 1GiB logical volume named "lvol" inside the "vgroup" volume group.
$ sudo lvcreate -L 1G -n lvol vgroup

4. Format the logical volume: You can use the mkfs.ext4

command to format the "lvol" logical volume with the ext4 filesystem.

```
$ sudo mkfs.ext4 /dev/vgroup/lvol
```

5. Mount the logical volume: You can use the mount command to mount the "lvol" logical volume on the "/lvol" directory. If the directory does not exist, you will need to create it first with mkdir.

```
$ sudo mkdir /lvol
$ sudo mount /dev/vgroup/lvol /lvol
```

6. Automatically mount at startup: To ensure the logical volume is mounted automatically at startup, you need to add an entry to the /etc/fstab file. The entry should look like this: /dev/vgroup/lvol /lvol ext4 defaults 0 0.

```
$ echo '/dev/vgroup/lvol /lvol ext4 defaults 0 0' | sudo tee -a /etc/fstab
```

7. Extend the filesystem: You can use the lvextend command to extend the "lvol" logical volume by 100M, and then use the resize2fs command to resize the filesystem to use the new space.

```
$ sudo lvextend -L +100M /dev/vgroup/lvol
$ sudo resize2fs /dev/vgroup/lvol
```

Question 27: Shell Scripting and User Input

As a system administrator, you are tasked with creating a shell script that can perform arithmetic operations. Your task is to:

1. Write a shell script named "sum.sh" located in the home directory.
2. The script should accept two integers as input from the user.
3. The script should calculate and print the sum of the two integers.
4. Ensure that the script checks if the user has entered exactly two arguments and if those arguments are integers.

Explanation

1. Create the script: You can use a text editor like nano or vi to create the script. The script should look like this:

```bash
#!/bin/bash

# Check if the user has entered exactly two arguments
if [ $# -ne 2 ]; then
    echo "Error: Please enter exactly two integers."
    exit 1
fi

# Check if the arguments are integers
if ! [[ $1 =~ ^-?[0-9]+$ ]] || ! [[ $2 =~ ^-?[0-9]+$ ]]; then
    echo "Error: Both arguments must be integers."
    exit 1
fi

# Calculate the sum
```

```
sum=$(($1 + $2))

# Print the sum
echo "The sum of $1 and $2 is $sum."
```

2. Save and close the file: Once you have entered the script, you can save and close the file. If you are using nano, you can press Ctrl+X to close the editor, Y to confirm that you want to save the changes, and Enter to confirm the file name.

3. Make the script executable: You can use the chmod command to make the script executable.
```
$ chmod +x ~/sum.sh
```

Question 28: File Searching and Copying

As a system administrator, you are tasked with managing files on a Linux server. Your task is to:

1. Find all files in the /etc directory that are larger than 5MB.
2. Copy these files to the /find/5mfiles directory.
3. Ensure that the /find/5mfiles directory exists before copying the files. If it doesn't exist, create it.

Explanation

1. Ensure the destination directory exists: You can use the mkdir -p command to create the /find/5mfiles directory if it doesn't already exist. The -p option makes mkdir create the directory and any necessary parent directories.

```
$ sudo mkdir -p /find/5mfiles
```

2. Find and copy the files: You can use the find command to find files in the /etc directory that are larger than 5MB. The -type f option tells find to only look for files, the -size +5M option tells find to only match files that are larger than 5MB, and the -exec cp {} /find/5mfiles \; part tells find to execute the cp command for each file found, copying it to the /find/5mfiles directory.

```
$ sudo find /etc -type f -size +5M -exec cp {} /find/5mfiles \;
```

Question 29: User Account Management and File Creation

As a system administrator, you are tasked with managing user accounts on a Linux server. Your task is to:

1. Configure the system such that every new user account created will have a file named "Welcome" in their home directory.
2. The "Welcome" file should contain a welcome message for the new user.

Explanation

1. Create the Welcome file: You can use a text editor like nano or vi to create the "Welcome" file in the /etc/skel directory. The file should contain a welcome message.
```
$ echo 'Welcome to our system!' | sudo tee /etc/skel/Welcome
```

2. Create a new user: When you create a new user with the useradd or adduser command (depending on your distribution), the system will copy the contents of the /etc/skel directory to the new user's home directory.

```
$ sudo useradd -m newuser
```
or
```
$ sudo adduser newuser
```

3. Verify the file is in the new user's home directory: You can use the ls command to verify that the "Welcome" file is in the new user's home directory.
```
$ ls /home/newuser
```

Question 30: User Account Management and Password Policies

As a system administrator, you are tasked with managing user accounts on a Linux server. Your task is to automate the process of setting the password expiry policy for all users so that:

1. All user passwords expire after 60 days.
2. The number of days after a password expires until the account is disabled.
3. The minimum number of days between password changes is 7 days.
4. The number of days of warning before a password expires is 7 days.
5. The expiration date of the user's account is unlimited.

Explanation

1. Automate the Process: To automate the process of setting the password expiry policy for all users, you can create a script that iterates over all user accounts and applies the changes using the chage command.

```
#!/bin/bash

for user in $(cut -d: -f1 /etc/passwd)
do
   sudo chage -M 60 -I 7 -m 7 -W 7 -E -1 $user
done
```

Save the script to a file ~/set_password_expiry.sh

2. Make it executable:

```
$ chmod +x ~/set_password_expiry.sh
```

3. Execute it with:
```
$ ~/set_password_expiry.sh
```

Explanation:

-M 60: Sets the maximum number of days a password is valid to 60 days.

-I 7: Sets the number of days after a password expires until the account is disabled. This value ensures that the account remains active for one week after the password expires.

-m 7: Sets the minimum number of days between password changes to 7 days.

-W 7: Sets the number of days of warning before a password expires to 7 days.

-E -1: Sets the expiration date of the user's account to be unlimited.

Replace username with the actual username of the user or use a wildcard * to apply changes to all users.

Verify Password Expiry Policy: To verify that the password expiry policy has been applied correctly, you can use the chage -l command to view the current password expiry information for a specific user:
```
$ sudo chage -l username
```
This command will display detailed information about the password expiry settings for the specified user.

Question 31: User and Group Management

In a Linux environment, create four users: alex, peter, carl, and dan. Once the users are created, perform the following tasks:

1. Add alex and peter to the accounting group, and carl and dan to the finance group.
2. Create shared group directories /groups/accounting and /groups/finance.
3. Change the owner group of the /groups/accounting directory to accounting, and the owner group of the /groups/finance directory to finance.
4. Grant the accounting and finance groups full access to their respective directories.
5. Ensure that other users do not have access to these directories.
6. Configure the system so that new files created in these directories inherit the group ownership of the directory.
7. Grant the finance group read and execute permissions on the /groups/accounting directory and all of its subdirectories and files.

Explanation

1. Create the users
```
$ useradd alex
$ useradd peter
$ useradd carl
$ useradd dan
```

2. Create the groups
```
$ groupadd accounting
$ groupadd finance
```

3. Add users to their respective groups
```
$ usermod -aG accounting alex
$ usermod -aG accounting peter
$ usermod -aG finance carl
$ usermod -aG finance dan
```

4. Create the shared directories
```
$ mkdir -p /groups/accounting
$ mkdir -p /groups/finance
```

5. Change the group ownership of the directories
```
$ chgrp accounting /groups/accounting
$ chgrp finance /groups/finance
```

6. Grant the groups full access to their directories
```
$ chmod 770 /groups/accounting
$ chmod 770 /groups/finance
```

7. Set the group ID for the directories so new files inherit group ownership
```
$ chmod g+s /groups/accounting
$ chmod g+s /groups/finance
```

8. Grant the finance group read and execute permissions on the accounting directory
```
$ setfacl -Rm g:finance:rx /groups/accounting
```

Explanation:

- The groupadd and useradd commands create the new groups and users, respectively.
- The usermod -aG command adds the users to their respective groups without removing them from any other groups they might belong to.
- The mkdir -p command creates the directories, making

parent directories as needed.

- The chgrp command changes the group ownership of the directories to the specified groups.

- The chmod 770 command grants full access (read, write, and execute permissions) to the owner and group, and no permissions to others.

- The chmod g+s command sets the setgid bit on the directories, which causes new files and subdirectories created within them to inherit their group ID.

- The setfacl command at the end grants the finance group read and execute permissions on the accounting directory and its contents. The -R option makes this change recursively, applying it to all subdirectories and files. The g:finance:rx argument specifies that the permissions (read and execute, denoted by rx) are being set for the finance group.

Question 32: SSH Configuration and Passwordless Login

In a Linux environment, specifically on a machine named Node4, set up SSH passwordless login for the root user. This will allow the root user to log in to Node4 without entering a password.

Explanation

1. Generate SSH Key Pair: If you haven't already done so, generate an SSH key pair for the root user. Use the following command to generate the key pair:

`$ ssh-keygen -t rsa`

Press Enter to accept the default file location (~/.ssh/id_rsa) and passphrase.

2. Copy Public Key to Node4: Use the ssh-copy-id command to copy the public key to the Node4 machine. Replace root@Node4 with the appropriate username and hostname if different:

`$ ssh-copy-id root@Node4`

You'll be prompted to enter the password for the root user on Node4. Once authenticated, the public key will be added to the authorized_keys file in the ~/.ssh directory of the root user on Node4.

3. Verify Passwordless Login: Attempt to SSH into Node4 as the root user:

`$ ssh root@Node4`

If the passwordless login setup was successful, you should be logged in to Node4 without being prompted for a password.

Question 33: SSH Security Best Practices and Root Login Configuration

In a Linux environment, specifically on a machine named Node3, configure the Secure Shell (SSH) service to permit root login. This will allow the root user to log in to Node3 via SSH.

Explanation

1. Backup SSH Configuration: Before making any changes, it's crucial to back up the SSH configuration file (sshd_config) to revert to the original settings if needed:
$ sudo cp /etc/ssh/sshd_config ssh/sshd_config_backup

2. Edit SSH Configuration: Edit the SSH server configuration file (sshd_config) using a text editor like nano or vim:
$ sudo vim ssh/sshd_config
Inside the file, locate the line that reads PermitRootLogin and change its value to yes:
PermitRootLogin yes

Save the changes and exit the text editor.

3. Restart SSH Service: After modifying the SSH configuration, restart the SSH service to apply the changes:
$ sudo systemctl restart sshd
This command reloads the SSH configuration and restarts the SSH service.

4. Test Root Login: Attempt to log in to Node3 via SSH as the root user:
$ ssh root@Node3
If the configuration was successful, you should be able to log in

as the root user without any issues.

Question 34: Docker Container Management and Image Handling

In a Linux environment, perform the following tasks related to Docker, a popular containerization tool:

1. Install Docker: Install the Docker package to enable container management.
2. Search for Official HTTPD Image: Use Docker to search for the official httpd (Apache HTTP Server) container image on Docker Hub.
3. Inspect HTTPD Image: Inspect the httpd image using Docker's inspect command to view detailed information about the image.
4. Pull HTTPD Image: Use Docker to pull (download) the httpd image from Docker Hub to your local machine.

Explanation

1. Install Docker: Install the Docker package using the appropriate package manager for your Linux distribution. For example, on Debian-based systems (such as Ubuntu), you can install Docker using the following commands:
```
$ sudo apt update
$ sudo apt install docker.io
```

On Red Hat-based systems (such as CentOS or RHEL), you can install Docker using:
```
$ sudo yum install docker
```

After installation, start and enable the Docker service:
```
$ sudo systemctl start docker
$ sudo systemctl enable docker
```

2. Search for Official HTTPD Image: Use Docker to search for the official httpd (Apache HTTP Server) container image on Docker Hub:

`$ docker search httpd`

This command will list all available httpd images on Docker Hub.

3. Inspect HTTPD Image: Inspect the httpd image using Docker's inspect command to view detailed information about the image:

`$ docker inspect httpd`

This command will display a JSON object containing detailed information about the httpd image, including its configuration, layers, and more.

4. Pull HTTPD Image: Use Docker to pull (download) the httpd image from Docker Hub to your local machine:

`$ docker pull httpd`

This command will download the latest version of the httpd image from Docker Hub to your local Docker repository.

Question 35: Bash Scripting and Command Line Interface (CLI) Operations

Write a bash script `~/actdate.sh` that saves the current date and time into a variable named actdate. The script should be distribution agnostic, meaning it should work on any Linux distribution. Additionally, the script should print the value of actdate to the console.

Explanation

1. Create the script:
Create the script `~/actdate.sh` with the following content:

```bash
#!/bin/bash

# Save the output of the 'date' command into the variable
'actdate'
actdate=$(date)

# Print the value of 'actdate'
echo "The current date and time is: $actdate"
```

Explanation:

- In this script, the date command is used to get the current date and time.
- The output of this command is saved into the actdate variable using command substitution $(command).
- This is a feature in bash where the output of the command inside the parentheses is used as the input for another command. In this case, the output of date is saved into actdate.
- The echo command is then used to print the value of actdate

to the console. The $actdate syntax is used to get the value of the actdate variable.
- The #!/bin/bash at the beginning of the script is called a shebang and it specifies that the script should be run using the bash shell. This ensures that the script will run correctly even if the user's default shell is not bash.

2. Make the script executable:
To make the script executable use:
$ chmod +x ~/actdate.sh
command before running it.

3. Run the script:
You can run the script using:
$ ~/actdate.sh

Question 36: Docker Containerization and Image Creation

Using Docker, create a Containerfile that builds an image named "are_you_ready". This image should be based on the Red Hat Universal Base Image 8 (ubi8/ubi). When a container is run from this image, it should display the message "Are You Ready?". After building the image, run a new container from the "are_you_ready" image and name it "are_you_ready_run".

Explanation

Here's a simple Containerfile that accomplishes the task:

```
# Use the Red Hat Universal Base Image 8 as the base image
FROM ubi8/ubi
```

```
# Use the 'echo' command to display "Are You Ready?" when the
container is run
CMD ["echo", "Are You Ready?"]
```

You can build the image with the following command:
```
$ docker build -t are_you_ready .
```

And you can run the container with the following command:
```
$ docker run --name are_you_ready_run are_you_ready
```

Explanation:

- In the Containerfile, the FROM directive is used to set the base image. In this case, the base image is the Red Hat Universal Base Image 8 (ubi8/ubi).
- The CMD directive is used to specify the command that

should be run when a container is started from the image. In this case, the echo command is used to display the message "Are You Ready?".

- The docker build command is used to build the image from the Containerfile. The -t option is used to name the image (are_you_ready), and the . specifies that the build context is the current directory (which should contain the Containerfile).

- The docker run command is used to start a new container from the image. The --name option is used to name the container (are_you_ready_run), and are_you_ready is the name of the image.

Question 37: Network File System (NFS) Configuration and Automounting with autofs

On a Linux system, configure autofs to automatically mount the "/home" directory of a remote NFS server at boot time. The remote NFS server's IP address is "192.168.1.100" and the exported directory is "/nfs/home". Ensure that the mount is accessible to all users on the local system. Also, verify the successful mount operation.

Explanation

1. Install autofs: Install autofs if it's not already installed on your system. Use your distribution's package manager to install autofs. For example, on Debian-based systems (such as Ubuntu), you can install autofs using the following command:
```
$ sudo apt update
$ sudo apt install autofs
```

On Red Hat-based systems (such as CentOS or RHEL), you can install autofs using:
```
$ sudo yum install autofs
```

2. Configure autofs: Edit the autofs configuration file (/etc/auto.master) to define the mount point and its configuration. Add the following line to the end of the file:
```
/home   /etc/auto.home
```
This line instructs autofs to mount the "/home" directory using the configuration defined in the /etc/auto.home file.

3. Create autofs map file: Create the autofs map file (/etc/auto.home) and define the mount options for the NFS share. Add the following line to the file:

```
* -fstype=nfs,rw,soft   192.168.1.100:/nfs/home
```
This line specifies that all directories under "/home" will be mounted using NFS from the remote server at "192.168.1.100" and the exported directory "/nfs/home".

4. Restart autofs service: Restart the autofs service to apply the changes:
```
$ sudo systemctl restart autofs
```

5. Verify mount operation: To verify that the NFS share is successfully mounted, navigate to the "/home" directory on your system and check if the remote directories are accessible:
```
$ ls /home
```
If the mount operation was successful, you should see the contents of the remote "/home" directory.

Question 38: Disk Management
and Bootloader Configuration

On a Linux system, overwrite the bootloader located on /dev/sda without overwriting the partition table or any data following it. Assume that the system uses the GRUB bootloader and that you have a copy of the desired bootloader in a file named bootloader.img. Also, verify the successful operation of the new bootloader.

Explanation

Use the dd command to overwrite the bootloader. The dd command is a powerful tool for copying and converting data. In this case, it's used to copy the contents of bootloader.img to /dev/sda:

```
$ sudo dd if=bootloader.img of=/dev/sda bs=446 count=1
```

Explanation:

- In this command, if=bootloader.img specifies the input file (bootloader.img), of=/dev/sda specifies the output file (/dev/sda), bs=446 sets the block size to 446 bytes, and count=1 specifies that only one block should be copied.
- The block size of 446 bytes is used because the bootloader is located in the first 446 bytes of the disk. The partition table and the rest of the data on the disk are located after the first 446 bytes, so they won't be overwritten.

LFCS PRACTICE
EXAM FOUR

Question 1: File Manipulation and Permissions Management

As a system administrator, you're tasked with completing the following objectives:

1. Text Shuffling: Shuffle the lines of a text file located at ~/shuffle.txt in a random order. Save the shuffled output to a new file at ~/shuffled_output.txt, ensuring that the original file remains unchanged.
2. Pattern Matching: Find all lines in a text file located at /var/log/syslog that contain the word "success". Additionally, count the number of these occurrences and redirect the output to a file named ~/success_count.txt in your home directory.
3. File Permissions: Modify the permissions of a file at ~/secret_file.txt to grant read and write access exclusively to the file's owner. Confirm the changes using an appropriate command.

Explanation

1. Text Shuffling: Use the shuf command to shuffle the lines of the text file located at ~/shuffle.txt and redirect the output to a new file at ~/shuffled_output.txt:
$ shuf ~/shuffle.txt > ~/shuffled_output.txt
This command shuffles the lines of the input file and saves the shuffled output to a new file while preserving the original file.

2. Pattern Matching: Use the grep command to find all lines in the text file located at /var/log/syslog that contain the word "success":
$ grep "success" /var/log/syslog > ~/success_count.txt
This command searches for lines containing the specified

pattern and redirects the output to a file named ~/success_count.txt.

To count the number of occurrences of the word "success", you can use the wc command:
`$ grep -c "success" /var/log/syslog`
This command counts the number of matching lines and prints the count to the terminal.

3. File Permissions: Modify the permissions of the file at ~/secret_file.txt to grant read and write access exclusively to the file's owner using the chmod command:
`$ chmod 600 ~/secret_file.txt`
This command sets the file permissions to rw-------, granting read and write access exclusively to the file's owner.

To confirm the changes, you can use the ls command with the -l option to display detailed information about the file, including its permissions:
`$ ls -l ~/secret_file.txt`
This command will display the file permissions, owner, group, and other metadata for the specified file.

Question 2: Web Server Installation and Configuration

You're tasked with installing the Apache web server on your machine, ensuring it's running, enabled to start on boot, and verifying the installation by accessing the Apache test page via a web browser.

Explanation

1. Install Apache: Use the package manager of your Linux distribution to install the Apache web server. For example, on Debian-based systems (such as Ubuntu), you can use the following command:
```
$ sudo apt update
$ sudo apt install apache2
```

On Red Hat-based systems (such as CentOS or RHEL), you can use:
```
$ sudo yum install httpd
```

2. Start Apache: After installation, start the Apache service using the appropriate command for your system's init system. For systems using systemd:
```
$ sudo systemctl start apache2    # For Debian-based systems
$ sudo systemctl start httpd      # For Red Hat-based systems
```
This command starts the Apache service.

3. Enable Apache to Start on Boot: To ensure that Apache starts automatically on system boot, enable the Apache service:
```
$ sudo systemctl enable apache2    # For Debian-based systems
$ sudo systemctl enable httpd      # For Red Hat-based systems
```
Enabling the service ensures that Apache will start automatically every time the system boots up.

4. Verify Apache Installation: Open a web browser on your local machine and enter the following URL in the address bar:
`$ http://localhost`

Alternatively, you can use the IP address of your machine if accessing from a remote system:
`$ http://<your_machine_ip>`
If Apache has been successfully installed and configured, you should see the default Apache test page.

Question 3: Automated Backup Management with Cron Jobs

You've been tasked with scheduling a cron job to execute a script named ~/weekly_backup.sh every Sunday at 3:00 AM. This script should back up the /var/www directory to a backup directory at ~/backups, ensuring the backup directory exists before execution. The script should also log its activity to a file named backup.log in the same directory.

Explanation

1. Create Backup Script: Create a backup script named weekly_backup.sh in your home directory (~/) using a text editor:
$ nano ~/weekly_backup.sh

Add the following content to the script:

```
#!/bin/bash

# Ensure backup directory exists
mkdir -p ~/backups

# Run backup and log activity
backup_date=$(date +"%Y-%m-%d_%H-%M-%S")
tar -czf ~/backups/www_backup_$backup_date.tar.gz /var/www > ~/backups/backup.log 2>&1
```

Save the file and exit the text editor.

2. Set Execution Permissions: Make the script executable by setting its execution permissions:
$ chmod +x ~/weekly_backup.sh

3. Schedule Cron Job: Open the crontab editor to schedule the cron job:
`$ crontab -e`

Add the following line to the crontab file to schedule the backup script to run every Sunday at 3:00 AM:
`0 3 * * 0 ~/weekly_backup.sh`
This cron schedule translates to: "At 3:00 AM every Sunday, execute the weekly_backup.sh script located in the user's home directory."

4. Save and Exit: Save the changes to the crontab file and exit the crontab editor.

5. Verification: To verify that the cron job has been successfully scheduled, you can list the configured cron jobs:
`$ crontab -l`
This command will display the contents of the crontab file, showing the scheduled cron job.

Question 4: User and
Group Management

You're tasked with creating a new user named "developer" with a home directory and a default shell. Additionally, add this user to the existing group "coders" and verify that the user has been successfully added to the group.

Explanation

1. Create a New User: Use the useradd command to create a new user named "developer" with a home directory and a default shell:

```
$ sudo useradd -m -s /bin/bash developer
```

-m: Create the user's home directory if it does not exist.
-s /bin/bash: Set the default shell for the user to /bin/bash.

2. Add User to Existing Group: Use the usermod command to add the user "developer" to the existing group "coders":

```
$ sudo usermod -aG coders developer
```

-aG: Append the user to the supplementary group(s) without removing the user from other groups.

3. Verify Group Membership: To verify that the user has been successfully added to the group "coders," you can use the groups command:

```
$ groups developer
```

This command will display all the groups that the user "developer" belongs to. The output should include the group "coders" if the user has been added successfully.

Question 5: User Account Creation and File Management

As a system administrator, you need to automate the process of providing new users with essential information upon account creation.

Task:

1. Configure Automatic File Placement: Set up the system to automatically create a welcome file ("README") in new user home directories.
2. Verify Configuration: Confirm the successful configuration by creating a test user and checking for the welcome file.

Explanation

1. Populate the Skel Directory:
$ echo "Welcome to our system! Please review the usage policy before starting." | sudo tee /etc/skel/README

sudo: Required for administrative tasks.
echo: Used to create the line to be appended.
"Welcome...": The content of the welcome message.
sudo tee /etc/skel/README: Creates the README file in the /etc/skel directory with the provided message.

2. Verification:

Create a Test User:
$ sudo useradd testuser

sudo: Required for administrative tasks.
useradd testuser: Creates a new user named "testuser".

Check for README File:
`$ sudo ls /home/testuser`

 # sudo: Required to access another user's home directory.
 # ls /home/testuser: Lists the contents of the test user's home directory. You should see "README" listed.

Explanation:

- The /etc/skel directory contains files and directories that are automatically copied to a new user's home directory when their account is created.
- Placing a file like "README" in this directory ensures its presence in all new user home directories.

Question 6: Automated System Updates with Bash Scripting

Design a bash script to automate the process of updating all installed packages on the system. The script should first refresh the package list, then upgrade the packages, and finally remove unnecessary packages. Additionally, ensure that the script logs its activities to a file named update.log in the home directory.

Explanation

1. Create the Bash Script: Use a text editor to create a bash script named update_packages.sh:
$ vim ~/update_packages.sh

Add the following content to the script:

```
#!/bin/bash

# Refresh package list
echo "Refreshing package list..."
sudo apt update > ~/update.log 2>&1   # For Debian-based systems
sudo yum update > ~/update.log 2>&1   # For Red Hat-based systems

# Upgrade packages
echo "Upgrading packages..."
sudo apt upgrade -y >> ~/update.log 2>&1 # For Debian-based systems
sudo yum upgrade -y >> ~/update.log 2>&1   # For Red Hat-based systems
```

```
# Remove unnecessary packages
echo "Removing unnecessary packages..."
sudo apt autoremove -y >> ~/update.log 2>&1  # For Debian-
based systems
sudo yum autoremove -y >> ~/update.log 2>&1  # For Red Hat-
based systems

echo "Update process completed."
```

Save the file and exit the text editor.

2. Set Execution Permissions: Make the script executable by setting its execution permissions:
`$ chmod +x ~/update_packages.sh`

3. Execute the Script: Run the script to update all installed packages on the system:
`$ ./update_packages.sh`
This will execute the script, which will refresh the package list, upgrade the packages, and remove unnecessary packages. The script will also log its activities to a file named update.log in the home directory.

4. Verification: You can verify the update process and check for any errors by examining the update.log file:
`$ cat ~/update.log`
This command will display the contents of the update.log file, showing the activities and any error messages encountered during the update process.

Question 7: Customizing Message of the Day (MOTD) with System Update Notifications

Implement a custom system-wide Message of the Day (MOTD) that includes information about available system updates. The message should be displayed to all users upon login, containing a welcoming message, the current date and time, and the number of available system updates. Ensure that the script updates the number of available updates every day at midnight.

Explanation

1. Create the MOTD Script: Use a text editor to create a bash script named update_motd.sh:
$ vim /etc/update_motd.sh

Add the following content to the script:

```
#!/bin/bash

# Get current date and time
datetime=$(date +"%A, %B %d, %Y %T")

# Get the number of available system updates
update_count=$(apt list --upgradable 2>/dev/null | grep -cE '^[0-9]+ packages')

# MOTD content
echo "Welcome to Our System"
echo "Current Date and Time: $datetime"
echo "Number of Available System Updates: $update_count"
```

Save the file and exit the text editor.

2. Set Execution Permissions: Make the script executable by setting its execution permissions:
$ chmod +x /etc/update_motd.sh

3. Update MOTD Configuration: Modify the MOTD configuration to execute the script and display its output upon user login:
$ echo "/etc/update_motd.sh" | sudo tee /etc/update-motd.d/10-update-motd
This command creates a symbolic link to the script in the /etc/update-motd.d/ directory, ensuring that it runs and updates the MOTD every time a user logs in.

4. Schedule Daily Update: Schedule the script to update the number of available system updates every day at midnight using cron:
$ sudo crontab -e

Add the following line to the crontab file to run the script daily at midnight:
0 0 * * * /etc/update_motd.sh
This cron schedule translates to: "At 12:00 AM every day, execute the /etc/update_motd.sh script."

5. Verification: To verify that the custom MOTD is displaying the correct information, log out of the system and log back in. The MOTD should display the welcoming message, current date and time, and the number of available system updates.

Question 8: Network Interface Management and DHCP Configuration

Retrieve and display the IP address, subnet mask, and broadcast address of the network interface eth0. Determine whether the interface is up and running. If it's not, provide the command to bring it up. Additionally, configure the system to automatically assign an IP address to eth0 using DHCP upon startup.

Explanation

1. Retrieve Network Interface Information: Use the ip command to retrieve information about the eth0 interface, including its IP address, subnet mask, and broadcast address:
`$ ip addr show eth0`
This command displays detailed information about the eth0 interface, including its IP address, subnet mask, and broadcast address.

2. Check Interface Status: Use the ip command to determine whether the eth0 interface is up and running:
`$ ip link show eth0`

If the interface is not up, you can bring it up using the following command:
`$ sudo ip link set eth0 up`
This command brings the eth0 interface up and enables it for network communication.

3. Configure DHCP for eth0: To configure the system to automatically assign an IP address to eth0 using DHCP upon startup, you need to modify the network configuration files.

The exact file to modify may vary depending on the Linux distribution.

A. Using systemd-networkd

For systems using systemd-networkd, create or modify the /etc/systemd/network/eth0.network file:
```
$ sudo nano /etc/systemd/network/eth0.network
```

Add the following lines to the file:

```
[Match]
Name=eth0

[Network]
DHCP=yes
```

Save the file and exit the text editor.

For systems using ifupdown, modify the /etc/network/interfaces file:

```
$ sudo nano /etc/network/interfaces
```

Add or modify the following lines in the file:

```
auto eth0
iface eth0 inet dhcp
```

Save the file and exit the text editor.

B. Using NetworkManager:

Use the nmcli command-line tool:
```
$ sudo nmcli connection modify eth0 ipv4.method dhcp
```

4. Restart Networking Service: After modifying the network configuration, restart the networking service to apply the changes:

For systemd-based systems:
```
$ sudo systemctl restart systemd-networkd
```

For systems using ifupdown:
```
$ sudo systemctl restart networking
```

Restart the NetworkManager service:
```
$ sudo systemctl restart NetworkManager
```
This command restarts the networking service, applying the new configuration for the eth0 interface.

Question 9: Automation and Configuration Management Challenge

Configure passwordless SSH login between two Linux servers, Node1 and Node2. Ensure that Node1 can SSH into Node2 without requiring a password.

Explanation

Step 1: Generate a key pair on Node1 (the client)
Use the ssh-keygen command to generate the key pair.
```
$ ssh-keygen
```

Step 2: Copy the public key to Node2 (the server)
Utilize the ssh-copy-id command to copy the public key to Node2.
```
$ ssh-copy-id user@node2
```

Step 3: Test the setup
Attempt to SSH from Node1 to Node2. It should not prompt for a password.
```
$ ssh user@node2
```

Explanation:

- In Step 1, a pair of cryptographic keys is generated on Node1 using the ssh-keygen command. By default, this command creates a private key (id_rsa) and a public key (id_rsa.pub) in the ~/.ssh directory of the current user's home directory.
- In Step 2, the public key is copied to Node2 using the ssh-copy-id command. This command appends the public key to the ~/.ssh/authorized_keys file on Node2, allowing Node1 to authenticate without a password.

- Finally, in Step 3, the setup is tested by attempting to SSH from Node1 to Node2 using the ssh command. If the setup was successful, Node1 should be able to SSH into Node2 without requiring a password.

Please note that this setup enables passwordless SSH from Node1 to Node2 only. If bidirectional passwordless SSH is desired, the steps must be repeated with the roles of Node1 and Node2 reversed. Additionally, ensure that the SSH service is running on both nodes. If not, start it with:
- For Ubuntu and other Debian-based distributions:
```
$ sudo systemctl start ssh
```
- For CentOS and other Red Hat-based distributions:
```
$ sudo systemctl start sshd
```

Question 10: Identify and terminate process with highest memory usage

Utilize the command line to list the running processes and determine the process with the highest memory usage. Ensure safe termination of this process, guaranteeing no data loss or corruption. Confirm that the process has been successfully terminated.

Explanation

$ ps aux --sort=-%mem | head -n 2
This command operates as follows:

ps is a command-line utility that displays information about active processes.
aux are options for ps that show all processes with a user-oriented format.
--sort=-%mem sorts processes by memory usage in descending order.
head -n 2 displays only the first two lines of output, which includes the column headers and the process with the highest memory usage.

The output reveals the process with the highest memory usage at the top, with its Process ID (PID) in the second column.

To safely terminate the process, you can utilize the kill command:
$ kill -9 [PID]
Replace [PID] with the actual Process ID. The -9 option instructs kill to send the SIGKILL signal, immediately terminating the process.

To verify termination of the process, you can employ the ps command once more:

```
$ ps -p [PID]
```

If the process has been successfully terminated, this command will not display any output. Conversely, if the process is still active, it will provide information about the process.

Question 11: Setting Up Host-based Intrusion Detection System (HIDS) with Tripwire

Task:

Utilize the command line to configure a host-based intrusion detection system (HIDS) like Tripwire. Set it up to monitor critical system files such as passwd, shadow, and hosts in the /etc/ directory, and send email alerts to the system administrator "admin@example.com" upon detecting changes. If any packages or services are required for this setup, please install them.

Explanation

Step 1: Install Tripwire (if not installed)

Install Tripwire:
If Tripwire is not installed on your system, install it using the appropriate package manager:

```
# For Debian/Ubuntu based systems
$ sudo apt-get install tripwire
```

```
# For CentOS/RHEL based systems
$ sudo yum install tripwire
```

Step 2: Initialize Tripwire Configuration

Initialize Tripwire Configuration:

Run the Tripwire configuration script to initialize the configuration files:

```
$ sudo tripwire-setup-keyfiles
```

Step 3: Configure Tripwire Policy

Edit Tripwire Policy Configuration:

Open the Tripwire policy configuration file for editing:
```
$ sudo nano /etc/tripwire/twpol.txt
```

Define Monitoring Targets:

Add the files to be monitored (e.g., passwd, shadow, hosts) in the /etc/ directory to the Tripwire policy configuration file:
```
/etc/passwd -> $(ReadOnly) ;
/etc/shadow -> $(ReadOnly) ;
/etc/hosts -> $(ReadOnly) ;
```

Step 4: Generate Tripwire Configuration

Generate Tripwire Configuration:

Generate the Tripwire configuration based on the updated policy:
```
$ sudo twadmin --create-polfile /etc/tripwire/twpol.txt
```

Step 5: Initialize Tripwire Database

Initialize Tripwire Database:

Initialize the Tripwire database to establish a baseline of system files:
```
$ sudo tripwire --init
```

Step 6: Schedule Tripwire Check

Schedule Tripwire Check:

Schedule Tripwire to perform periodic checks and send email alerts upon detecting changes:

```
$ sudo crontab -e
```

Add the following line to schedule a daily Tripwire check:

```
0 0 * * * /usr/sbin/tripwire --check
```

Step 7: Configure Email Alerts

Configure Email Alerts:

Configure Tripwire to send email alerts to the system administrator:

Edit the Tripwire configuration file:

```
$ sudo nano /etc/tripwire/twcfg.txt
```

Set the EMAILREPORTLEVEL to a value that includes email alerts:

```
EMAILREPORTLEVEL = 3
```

Set the EMAILTO to the system administrator's email address:

```
EMAILTO = admin@example.com
```

Question 12: Essential Git
Commands Challenge

Execute the following tasks using Git commands:

1. Cloning a Git Repository: Clone a Git repository from the URL https://github.com/tom/repo.git.
2. Establishing a New Branch: Create a new branch named feature in the cloned repository.
3. Switching Branches: Switch to the newly created feature branch.
4. Merging Branches: Merge the feature branch into the master branch.

Explanation

1. Cloning a Git Repository: To clone a Git repository from the given URL, utilize the git clone command:
`$ git clone https://github.com/tom/repo.git`
This command generates a local copy of the repository at the current location.

2. Establishing a New Branch: Create a new branch named feature in the cloned repository using the git branch command:
`$ git branch feature`
This command establishes a new branch named feature.

3. Switching Branches: Switch to the newly created feature branch with the git checkout command:
`$ git checkout feature`
This command adjusts the working directory to the feature branch.

4. Merging Branches: To merge the feature branch into the master branch, first switch to the master branch and then employ the git merge command:

```
$ git checkout master
$ git merge feature
```

These commands navigate the working directory to the master branch and subsequently merge the changes from the feature branch into the master branch.

Question 13: User Account Management and Security

As a system administrator, you are required to manage user accounts on a Linux server. Your task is to create a new user named Sam with a User ID (UID) of 1500. However, for security reasons, Sam should not have access to any interactive shell on the system.

Explanation

1. To create a new user named Sam with a UID of 1500 and no shell access, use the following command:
$ sudo useradd -u 1500 -s /usr/sbin/nologin Sam

The -u option sets the user ID, and the -s option sets the login shell. The /usr/sbin/nologin shell prevents the user from logging into the system.

2. To verify the changes, use the following command:
$ grep Sam /etc/passwd
This command displays the user information for Sam's account.

Explanation:

- In Linux, the useradd command is used to create a new user or update default new user information.
- The -u option is used to set the user ID, and the -s option is used to set the login shell.
- The /usr/sbin/nologin shell is a special shell assigned to the user's account to prevent the user from logging into the system. This is a common practice to enhance the security of user accounts.

- The grep command is used to check the user information in the passwd file, which contains all the local user information.

Question 14: File System Links

On a Linux server, your task is to create a hard link and a symbolic link to a file named "data.txt". The original file is located in the /home/$USER/ directory. The hard link should be created in the same directory as the original file, while the symbolic link should be created in the /var/tmp/ directory.

Explanation

1. Create a hard link to "data.txt" in the same directory:
```
$ ln /home/$USER/data.txt /home/$USER/data_hardlink.txt
```

2. Create a symbolic link to "data.txt" in the /var/tmp/ directory:
```
$ ln -s /home/$USER/data.txt /var/tmp/data_symlink.txt
```

3. To verify that the links have been correctly created, you can use the ls command with the -l option, which displays file information including the target of symbolic links:
```
$ ls -l /home/$USER/data_hardlink.txt /var/tmp/data_symlink.txt
```
This command should show that "data_hardlink.txt" is a regular file (indicating that it's a hard link) and that "data_symlink.txt" is a symbolic link to "/home/$USER/data.txt".

Question 15: Search and Append Text to a File

Your task is to find occurrences of the string "blank" in the "passwd" file located in the "/etc/" directory on a Linux server. After locating these occurrences, append them to the file "/home/blankword". It's important to note that the existing content of the "/home/blankword" file should not be removed.

Explanation

1. Search for Occurrences: Use the grep command to search for occurrences of the string "blank" in the "passwd" file:
`$ sudo grep "blank" /etc/passwd`
This command searches for the string "blank" in the "passwd" file located in the "/etc/" directory.

2. Append to "/home/blankword" File: To append the search results to the "/home/blankword" file, use the tee command with the "-a" option to append to a file instead of overwriting it:
`$ sudo grep "blank" passwd | sudo tee -a /home/blankword`
This command pipes the output of the grep command to tee, which appends it to the "/home/blankword" file.

3. Verify the Content: To verify that the occurrences of "blank" have been successfully appended to the "/home/blankword" file, you can use the cat command:
`$ cat /home/blankword`
This command displays the content of the "/home/blankword" file, including the appended occurrences of "blank".

Question 16: File System and Directory Management

On a Linux server, your task is to create a directory hierarchy that includes the directories /V1, /V1/V2, and /V1/V2/V3.

Explanation

To create a directory hierarchy, you would typically use the mkdir command with the -p option, which creates parent directories as needed. Here are the steps:

1. Run the mkdir command with the -p option to create the directory hierarchy:
```
$ sudo mkdir -p /V1/V2/V3
```

2. To verify that the directory hierarchy has been correctly created, you can use the ls command:
```
$ ls -R /V1
```

This command should output:

```
/V1:
V2

/V1/V2:
V3

/V1/V2/V3:
```

This confirms that the directory hierarchy /V1/V2/V3 has been correctly created.

Question 17: Restricting Crontab Access for Specific Users

Your task involves modifying the system configuration on a Linux server named Node3 to prevent all users from using the crontab command, except for the user named tom.

Explanation

To restrict crontab access for all users except the user named "tom" on Node3 in a distribution-agnostic approach, follow these steps:

1. Editing /etc/cron.allow File: The /etc/cron.allow file is used to specify users who are allowed to use the crontab command. If this file exists, only users listed in it can create or modify their own cron jobs. If it doesn't exist, all users can use crontab unless their username appears in /etc/cron.deny.

Since you want to allow only the user "tom" to use crontab, you need to create or edit the /etc/cron.allow file and add "tom" to it.

```
$ sudo echo "tom" > /etc/cron.allow
```

This command creates or edits the /etc/cron.allow file and adds "tom" to it.

2. Editing /etc/cron.deny File (Optional): It's also a good practice to ensure that the /etc/cron.deny file does not contain any users you want to restrict from using crontab. You can remove any entries from this file if necessary.

```
$ sudo rm -f /etc/cron.deny
```

This command removes the /etc/cron.deny file if it exists.

3. Verify Restrictions: To verify that crontab access has been

restricted for all users except "tom", try accessing crontab with a non-privileged user account:

```
$ crontab -e
```

You should receive a message indicating that you are not allowed to use crontab.

4. Verify Access for "tom": Finally, log in as the user "tom" and verify that crontab access is allowed:

```
$ su - tom
```
```
$ crontab -e
```

You should be able to edit the crontab file without any restrictions.

Question 18: Kernel and Process Management

As a system administrator, you're tasked with various process management responsibilities:

1. CPU Usage: Identify and list the top 5 processes consuming the most CPU resources.
2. Termination of Processes: Terminate the process utilizing the highest CPU resources.
3. Memory Usage: Identify and list the top 5 processes consuming the most memory resources.
4. Process Information: Display detailed information about the process using the highest amount of CPU.

Explanation

1. CPU Usage:

To identify and list the top 5 processes consuming the most CPU resources, use the top command:
```
$ top -b -n1 | head -n 12 | tail -n 5
```

2. Termination of Processes:

To terminate the process consuming the highest amount of CPU, first, identify its PID using the ps command:
```
$ ps aux --sort=-%cpu | head -n 2
```
This command displays the process with the highest CPU usage at the top. Once you have the PID, terminate the process using the kill command:
```
$ sudo kill -9 <PID>
```
Replace <PID> with the actual Process ID.

3. Memory Usage:

To identify and list the top 5 processes consuming the most memory resources, utilize the ps command:
`$ ps aux --sort=-%mem | head -n 6`

4. Process Information:

To display detailed information about the process utilizing the highest amount of CPU, use the ps command with the -F option:
`$ ps -F <PID>`
Replace <PID> with the actual Process ID.

Question 19: Process Management and Resource Cleanup

You're tasked with identifying the process consuming the most memory on the system, displaying its PID, user, command, and memory usage. Then, safely terminate this process, ensuring that it has a chance to clean up resources. Additionally, provide a command to prevent this process from restarting automatically.

Explanation

1. Identify Process Consuming Most Memory: Use the top command to identify the process consuming the most memory on the system:

`$ top -o %MEM -n 1`

This command sorts the processes based on memory usage (%MEM) and displays the top process consuming the most memory.

2. Display Process Information: Note down the PID (Process ID), user, command, and memory usage of the identified process.

3. Terminate the Process: Use the kill command to safely terminate the identified process:

`$ sudo kill -15 <PID>`

The -15 option sends a SIGTERM signal to the process, allowing it to gracefully terminate and clean up resources.

4. Prevent Automatic Restart: To prevent the terminated process from automatically restarting, you can use the systemctl command to stop and disable its associated service:

`$ sudo systemctl stop <service_name>`

```
$ sudo systemctl disable <service_name>
```

Replace <service_name> with the name of the service associated with the terminated process.

5. Verify Termination: After terminating the process and preventing its automatic restart, you can verify that the process has stopped using the ps command:

```
$ ps -p <PID>
```

If the process is no longer running, you will not see any output.

Question 20: Storage Management and System Monitoring

1. Storage Management: Create a new partition on the disk /dev/sdd with a size of 300MB, assign it the partition number 1 (making it /dev/sdd1), and format it with the ext4 filesystem. After formatting, mount the partition at a directory /mnt/new_partition. Ensure that the partition is automatically mounted at this location upon system reboot. Also, provide the command to verify the successful creation and mounting of the new partition.

2. System Monitoring: Monitor the system's CPU and memory usage in real-time. Display a breakdown of CPU usage by different processes and threads. Also, show the memory usage of each process. Provide a command to sort the processes by their CPU and memory usage.

Explanation

1. Storage Management:

To create a new partition, format it with the ext4 filesystem, mount it at /mnt/new_partition, and ensure automatic mounting upon system reboot, follow these steps:

```
# Create a new partition on /dev/sdd with a size of 300MB
$ sudo parted /dev/sdd mkpart primary ext4 0% 300MB
```

```
# Format the partition with the ext4 filesystem
$ sudo mkfs.ext4 /dev/sdd1
```

```
# Create a mount point
$ sudo mkdir -p /mnt/new_partition
```

Mount the partition at /mnt/new_partition
```
$ sudo mount /dev/sdd1 /mnt/new_partition
```

Add an entry to /etc/fstab for automatic mounting
```
$ echo "/dev/sdd1 /mnt/new_partition ext4 defaults 0 2" | sudo tee -a /etc/fstab
```

To verify the successful creation and mounting of the new partition, use the following command:
```
$ df -hT | grep /mnt/new_partition
```
This command should display information about the mounted partition, including its filesystem type and size.

2. System Monitoring:

To monitor CPU and memory usage in real-time, display a breakdown of CPU usage by different processes and threads, and show the memory usage of each process, follow these steps:

Monitor CPU and memory usage in real-time
```
$ top
```

Sort processes by CPU usage
```
$ top -o %CPU
```

Sort processes by memory usage
```
$ top -o %MEM
```
The top command provides real-time monitoring of system resources, including CPU and memory usage. By default, it displays a list of processes sorted by CPU usage. Adding the -o %CPU option sorts the processes by CPU usage, while -o %MEM sorts them by memory usage.

Question 21: Archives
and Encryption

You're tasked with creating a zip archive of the entire /home/tom directory, ensuring that the archive maintains the original file permissions and ownership. Then, encrypt the archive using GPG with a secure passphrase. Move the encrypted archive to the /backup directory and verify the integrity of the moved, encrypted archive.

Explanation

1. Create a Zip Archive: Use the zip command to create a zip archive of the /home/tom directory:
`$ zip -r /tmp/tom_backup.zip /home/tom`
This command creates a zip archive named tom_backup.zip containing the entire /home/tom directory recursively (-r option), preserving file permissions and ownership.

2. Encrypt the Archive using GPG: Encrypt the zip archive using GPG with a secure passphrase:
`$ gpg --output /tmp/tom_backup.zip.gpg --symmetric /tmp/tom_backup.zip`
This command encrypts the tom_backup.zip archive using symmetric encryption, prompting you to enter a passphrase.

3. Move the Encrypted Archive to the Backup Directory: Move the encrypted archive to the /backup directory:
`$ mv /tmp/tom_backup.zip.gpg /backup/`
This command moves the encrypted archive to the /backup directory.

4. Verify the Integrity of the Encrypted Archive: To verify the integrity of the moved, encrypted archive, you can use GPG to

decrypt it and then compare the checksums:

```
$ gpg --output /tmp/decrypted.zip --decrypt /backup/
tom_backup.zip.gpg
$ sha256sum /tmp/tom_backup.zip
$ sha256sum /tmp/decrypted.zip
```

Compare the checksums generated by the sha256sum command. If they match, the integrity of the encrypted archive is verified.

Question 22: File Management and Automated Monitoring

You're tasked with finding and listing all files in the /var/log directory that have been modified in the last 5 days. Display the file name, modification time, and size in human-readable format. Additionally, provide a command to monitor the /var/log directory and automatically list newly modified files every day at midnight.

Explanation

1. Find and List Recently Modified Files: Use the find command to locate files in the /var/log directory that have been modified in the last 5 days. Then, use the ls command to display the file name, modification time, and size in a human-readable format:

```
$ find /var/log -type f -mtime -5 -exec ls -lh {} +
```

This command finds all files (-type f) in the /var/log directory that have been modified within the last 5 days (-mtime -5) and displays their details using ls -lh.

2. Automate Monitoring with Cron: To automatically list newly modified files in the /var/log directory every day at midnight, you can create a cron job. Edit the cron table using the crontab -e command and add the following line:

```
0 0 * * * find /var/log -type f -mtime -1 -exec ls -lh {} +
```

This cron job runs the specified command (finding and listing newly modified files) at midnight (0 minute, 0 hour) every day (0 0 * * *).

Question 23: System Information Retrieval and Display

Write a shell script system_info.sh that retrieves and displays the following system information:

1. Kernel version
2. System uptime
3. Number of currently logged-in users
4. Total number of running processes

Explanation

1. Create the system_info.sh shell script with the following content:

```
#!/bin/bash

# Retrieve and display kernel version
kernel_version=$(uname -r)
echo "Kernel Version: $kernel_version"

# Retrieve and display system uptime
uptime=$(uptime -p)
echo "System Uptime: $uptime"

# Retrieve and display number of currently logged-in users
logged_in_users=$(who | wc -l)
echo "Number of Logged-in Users: $logged_in_users"

# Retrieve and display total number of running processes
running_processes=$(ps -e --no-headers | wc -l)
echo "Total Number of Running Processes: $running_processes"
```

Save and exit.

2. Make it executable using chmod +x system_info.sh.

Explanation:

Kernel Version:
- uname -r command retrieves the kernel version.
- The output is stored in the variable kernel_version.

System Uptime:
- uptime -p command retrieves the system uptime in a human-readable format.
- The output is stored in the variable uptime.

Number of Logged-in Users:
- who | wc -l command lists all logged-in users, and wc -l counts the lines.
- The output is stored in the variable logged_in_users.

Total Number of Running Processes:
- ps -e --no-headers command lists all running processes without headers, and wc -l counts the lines.
- The output is stored in the variable running_processes.
- Each piece of system information is then displayed with an appropriate message using echo.

Question 24: Automated Network Configuration

Create a shell script named "~/network_configurator.sh" to perform the following networking tasks:

1. Configure a static IP address (192.168.1.100) for the network interface eth1.
2. Set the netmask to 255.255.255.0 and the gateway to 192.168.1.1.
3. Ensure proper DNS resolution by setting the DNS server to 8.8.8.8.
4. Ensure these settings persist across reboots.

Explanation

1. Create the network_configurator.sh script with the following contents:

```bash
#!/bin/bash

# Define network configuration variables
INTERFACE="eth1"
IP_ADDRESS="192.168.1.100"
NETMASK="255.255.255.0"
GATEWAY="192.168.1.1"
DNS_SERVER="8.8.8.8"

# Configure static IP address for eth1
cat    <<EOF    >    /etc/sysconfig/network-scripts/ifcfg-$INTERFACE
TYPE=Ethernet
BOOTPROTO=static
NAME=$INTERFACE
```

```
DEVICE=$INTERFACE
ONBOOT=yes
IPADDR=$IP_ADDRESS
NETMASK=$NETMASK
GATEWAY=$GATEWAY
DNS1=$DNS_SERVER
EOF

# Restart network service to apply changes
$ systemctl restart network
```

Save this script as network_configurator.sh in the user's home directory (~/). Make it executable using chmod +x ~/ network_configurator.sh.

Explanation:

1. Define Network Configuration Variables:
- Variables are defined for the network interface (INTERFACE), IP address (IP_ADDRESS), netmask (NETMASK), gateway (GATEWAY), and DNS server (DNS_SERVER).

2. Configure Static IP Address:
- Using a here document (cat <<EOF > /etc/sysconfig/network-scripts/ifcfg-$INTERFACE), the script writes network configuration settings to the interface's configuration file.
- Settings include type, boot protocol (static), interface name, device, on boot status, IP address, netmask, gateway, and DNS server.

3. Restart Network Service:
- The script restarts the network service (systemctl restart network) to apply the changes.

Question 25: Automated
Storage Management

Create a shell script storage_manager.sh to execute the following tasks:

1. Reduce the size of the logical volume named mylv within the volume group myvg by 50MB.
2. Ensure the corresponding file system on the logical volume is resized accordingly.
3. Verify the successful changes.

Explanation

1. Create the shell script with the following content:

```bash
#!/bin/bash

# Define variables
LV_NAME="mylv"
VG_NAME="myvg"
REDUCE_AMOUNT="50" # MB

# Reduce logical volume size
lvreduce -L "-${REDUCE_AMOUNT}M" "/dev/$VG_NAME/$LV_NAME"

# Resize the file system on the logical volume
resize2fs "/dev/$VG_NAME/$LV_NAME"

# Verify changes
lvdisplay "/dev/$VG_NAME/$LV_NAME"
```

Save this script as storage_manager.sh. Make it executable

using chmod +x storage_manager.sh.

Explanation:

1. Define Variables:
- Variables are defined for the logical volume name (LV_NAME), volume group name (VG_NAME), and the amount to reduce the logical volume size (REDUCE_AMOUNT).

2. Reduce Logical Volume Size:
- The lvreduce command is used to reduce the size of the logical volume by the specified amount (-L "-${REDUCE_AMOUNT}M").

3. Resize File System:
- The resize2fs command is used to resize the file system on the logical volume to match the reduced volume size.

4. Verify Changes:
- Finally, the lvdisplay command is used to display detailed information about the logical volume, including its size, confirming that the changes were applied successfully.

Question 26: Automated Git Operations Scripting

Write a shell script git_operations.sh to execute the following essential Git operations:

1. Clone a specific repository from GitHub.
2. Create a new branch in the cloned repository.
3. Make changes to a file test in the new branch.
4. Commit the changes with a meaningful commit message.
5. Push the changes to the remote repository.
6. Ensure script reusability for different repositories and branches.

Variables:

REPO_URL="https://github.com/max/repository.git"
BRANCH_NAME="new-branch"
FILE_PATH="~/test"
COMMIT_MESSAGE="Welcome to LFCS practice"

Explanation

1. Create a shell script git_operations.sh with the following content:

```
#!/bin/bash

# Variables
REPO_URL="https://github.com/max/repository.git"
BRANCH_NAME="new-branch"
FILE_PATH="~/test"
COMMIT_MESSAGE="Welcome to LFCS practice"
```

```
# Clone repository
git clone $REPO_URL
cd repository

# Create and switch to new branch
git checkout -b $BRANCH_NAME

# Make changes to the file
echo "LFCS practice changes" >> $FILE_PATH

# Stage changes
git add $FILE_PATH

# Commit changes
git commit -m "$COMMIT_MESSAGE"

# Push changes to remote repository
git push origin $BRANCH_NAME
```

Save this script as git_operations.sh and make it executable using chmod +x git_operations.sh.

Explanation:

1. Clone Repository:
The git clone command clones the repository specified by REPO_URL into the current directory.
2. Create and Switch to New Branch:
The git checkout -b command creates a new branch ($BRANCH_NAME) and switches to it.
3. Make Changes to File:
Changes are made to the file specified by FILE_PATH using standard file manipulation commands.
4. Stage Changes:
The git add command stages the changes made to the file for commit.

5. Commit Changes:

The git commit command commits the staged changes with the commit message specified by COMMIT_MESSAGE.

6. Push Changes to Remote Repository:

The git push command pushes the committed changes to the remote repository on the specified branch.

Question 27: Firewall Rule Configuration for Secure Communication

As a system administrator, you're tasked with configuring the firewall on your server. Your goal is to create a shell script firewall_config.sh to implement a firewall rule allowing incoming traffic on TCP port 443, commonly used for HTTPS connections.

Explanation

1. Create the script firewall_config.sh with the following content:

```
#!/bin/bash

# Variables
PORT_NUMBER="443"

# Allow incoming traffic on TCP port 443
iptables -A INPUT -p tcp --dport $PORT_NUMBER -j ACCEPT

# Save the iptables rules to persist across reboots
iptables-save > /etc/iptables/rules.v4
```

Save this script as firewall_config.sh and make it executable using chmod +x firewall_config.sh.

Explanation:

1. Define Variables:
The PORT_NUMBER variable is set to 443, representing the TCP port used for HTTPS connections.

2. Allow Incoming Traffic:

The iptables -A INPUT -p tcp --dport $PORT_NUMBER -j ACCEPT command appends a rule to the INPUT chain of the firewall, allowing incoming TCP traffic on port 443.

3. Persist Firewall Rules:

The iptables-save > /etc/iptables/rules.v4 command saves the current iptables rules to the /etc/iptables/rules.v4 file, ensuring that the firewall configuration persists across reboots.

Question 28: System Troubleshooting and Optimization

1. Disk Space Troubleshooting: Your system is experiencing low disk space on the root filesystem (/), potentially affecting system functionality. Efficiently identify the directories consuming the most space and implement solutions to mitigate the issue while ensuring system stability.

2. DNS Resolution Troubleshooting: Your system is encountering difficulties accessing external websites due to DNS resolution issues. Thoroughly investigate the root cause of the problem and implement a permanent solution that rectifies the DNS resolution problem without disrupting other network configurations.

Explanation

1. Disk Space Troubleshooting:

To identify directories consuming the most space, use the du command to display disk usage statistics for each directory in the root filesystem:

```
$ du -h --max-depth=1 / | sort -rh
```

This command lists directories in descending order of disk usage, allowing you to pinpoint which directories are taking up the most space. Common culprits include /var/log, /var/cache, and /home.

Once identified, you can free up space by:

- Deleting unnecessary files or logs.
- Moving large files to another filesystem.
- Clearing package cache using apt clean or yum clean all.

- Truncating log files using truncate or logrotate.

2. DNS Resolution Troubleshooting:

Start by checking the /etc/resolv.conf file to ensure it contains valid DNS server configurations. You can use commands like cat /etc/resolv.conf or nmcli dev show | grep DNS to verify DNS settings.

Test DNS resolution using the nslookup or dig command to diagnose DNS resolution problems:
$ nslookup example.com
or
$ dig example.com

If DNS resolution is unsuccessful, verify network connectivity and DNS server availability. Ensure that the DNS servers specified in /etc/resolv.conf are reachable and functioning correctly.

Consider using alternative DNS servers such as Google DNS (8.8.8.8 and 8.8.4.4) or Cloudflare DNS (1.1.1.1 and 1.0.0.1) by updating the /etc/resolv.conf file.

To make DNS server changes permanent, update the /etc/resolv.conf file or configure DNS settings in network configuration files such as /etc/network/interfaces or /etc/sysconfig/network-scripts/ifcfg-* depending on your distribution.

Question 29: Containerized Database Management with Docker

You've been tasked with setting up a MySQL server using Docker for a new project. Execute the following steps to accomplish the task:

1. Install Docker:
Ensure Docker is installed on your system and configured to start on boot if not already done.

2. Download MySQL Image:
Pull the official MySQL image from Docker Hub and verify its successful download.

3. Launch MySQL Container:
Initiate a MySQL container named "dbserver," ensuring it's configured to start automatically on system boot. Additionally, verify the ability to connect to the MySQL server from within the container.

Explanation

1. Install Docker:
If Docker is not already installed, you can install it using distribution-specific package managers like apt, yum, or dnf. For example, on Ubuntu:
```
$ sudo apt update
$ sudo apt install docker.io
```

Enable Docker to start on boot:
```
$ sudo systemctl enable docker
$ sudo systemctl start docker
```

2. Download MySQL Image:

Pull the official MySQL image from Docker Hub:
`$ docker pull mysql`

Verify the successful download by listing Docker images:
`$ docker images`

3. Launch MySQL Container:

Launch a MySQL container named "dbserver" with specific configurations:
`$ docker run -d --name dbserver -e`
`MYSQL_ROOT_PASSWORD=my-secret-pw -p 3306:3306 mysql`

-*d:* Run the container in detached mode.
--name dbserver: Assign the name "dbserver" to the container.
-e MYSQL_ROOT_PASSWORD=my-secret-pw: Set the MySQL root password.
-p 3306:3306: Map the container's MySQL port to the host's port for external access.

Verify the container is running:
`$ docker ps`

Test connectivity to the MySQL server from within the container:
`$ docker exec -it dbserver mysql -uroot -p`
This command opens a MySQL client shell within the container, allowing you to execute SQL commands.

Question 30: Network Troubleshooting and Optimization

You're confronted with intermittent network connectivity issues. Your objective is to pinpoint the root cause of these disruptions and implement a permanent solution without adversely affecting other network configurations.

Explanation

1. Check Network Hardware:

- Ensure all network cables are securely connected to their respective ports on networking devices (routers, switches, etc.).
- Verify that networking devices such as routers and switches are powered on and functioning correctly. Check for any error lights or indicators on these devices.

2. Test Network Connectivity:

- Use the ping command to test connectivity to known network resources such as routers, servers, or websites:
$ ping -c 4 google.com
This command sends ICMP echo requests to the specified destination and waits for responses, indicating network connectivity.

- Check for packet loss, high latency, or inconsistent response times, which may indicate network issues.

2. Check Network Configuration:

- Review network configuration files such as /etc/network/

interfaces or /etc/sysconfig/network-scripts/ifcfg-* to ensure correct network settings, including IP address, subnet mask, gateway, and DNS servers.
- Use tools like ifconfig, ip addr, or nmcli to check the current network configuration of network interfaces.

3. Investigate Network Services:

- Check the status of network services such as DHCP, DNS, and firewalls to ensure they are running correctly and not causing disruptions.
- Review log files (e.g., /var/log/syslog, /var/log/messages) for any errors or warnings related to network services.

4. Update Network Drivers and Firmware:

- Ensure that network interface drivers and firmware are up to date. Outdated drivers or firmware can lead to compatibility issues and network disruptions.
- Use distribution-specific package managers (e.g., apt, yum, zypper) to update network-related packages.

5. Implement Permanent Solutions:

Based on the investigation, implement permanent solutions such as:

- Adjusting network configuration settings.
- Restarting or reconfiguring network services.
- Upgrading hardware components if necessary.
- Implementing quality of service (QoS) policies to prioritize network traffic.

6. Monitor Network Performance:

- Set up network monitoring tools or services to continuously

monitor network performance and detect any future issues proactively.
- Utilize tools like iftop, nload, or Wireshark to monitor network traffic and identify potential bottlenecks.

Question 31: Web Server
Setup and Virtual Hosting

You're tasked with setting up a web server for a new project. Follow the steps below to accomplish this:

1. Install Nginx: Ensure Nginx is installed on your system and configured to start automatically on boot if not already done.
2. Configure Virtual Host: Set up a virtual host for the website "example.com" with its document root located at /var/www/example. Verify the correctness of the configuration and successfully reload the Nginx service with the updated settings.

Explanation

1. Install Nginx: First, ensure that the system package repositories are up to date:
$ sudo apt update   # For Debian/Ubuntu
$ sudo yum update   # For CentOS/RHEL

Then, install Nginx using the package manager:
$ sudo apt install nginx   # For Debian/Ubuntu
$ sudo yum install nginx   # For CentOS/RHEL

2. Configure Virtual Host: Navigate to the Nginx configuration directory:
$ cd /etc/nginx/sites-available

Create a new configuration file for the virtual host:
$ sudo nano example.com

Add the following configuration, replacing example.com with your domain name:

```
server {
  listen 80;
  listen [::]:80;

  server_name example.com www.example.com;

  root /var/www/example;
  index index.html index.htm;

  location / {
    try_files $uri $uri/ =404;
  }
}
```

Save the file and exit the text editor.

3. Enable the Virtual Host: Create a symbolic link to enable the virtual host configuration:
```
$ sudo ln -s /etc/nginx/sites-available/example.com /etc/nginx/sites-enabled/
```

4. Verify Configuration: Check the syntax of the Nginx configuration to ensure there are no errors:
```
$ sudo nginx -t
```

If the syntax is OK, reload Nginx to apply the changes:
```
$ sudo systemctl reload nginx
```

5. Document Root Setup: Create the document root directory for the virtual host:
```
$ sudo mkdir -p /var/www/example
```

Set appropriate permissions for the directory:
```
$ sudo chown -R www-data:www-data /var/www/example
$ sudo chmod -R 755 /var/www/example
```

6. Test the Website: Create a simple index.html file in the document root directory to test the virtual host:
$ echo "Welcome to example.com" | sudo tee /var/www/ example/index.html

7. Final Verification: Open a web browser and navigate to http://example.com. You should see the "Welcome to example.com" message, confirming that the virtual host is correctly configured and serving content.

Question 32: Database Management

Your current task involves setting up a new database. Follow the steps below to achieve this:

1. Connect to MariaDB Server: Connect to the MariaDB server installed on your system. Verify successful login and the ability to execute SQL commands.
2. Create New Database: Generate a new database named "companydb." Confirm the creation of the database.
3. Create New User: Create a new user named "dbuser" with the password "dbpass," ensuring the user possesses the requisite privileges to execute operations on the "companydb" database.

Explanation

1. Connect to MariaDB Server: Ensure that MariaDB server is installed and running on your system. Use the appropriate command to login to the MariaDB server as the root user:
```
$ mysql -u root -p
```
You will be prompted to enter the root password.

2. Create New Database: Once logged in to MariaDB, execute the following SQL command to create the "companydb" database:
```
CREATE DATABASE companydb;
```

You can verify the creation of the database by listing all databases:
```
SHOW DATABASES;
```

3. Create New User: Next, create a new user named "dbuser" with the password "dbpass" and grant it all privileges on the "companydb" database:

```
CREATE USER 'dbuser'@'localhost' IDENTIFIED BY 'dbpass';
GRANT ALL PRIVILEGES ON companydb.* TO
'dbuser'@'localhost';
FLUSH PRIVILEGES;
```

This creates a new user "dbuser" with the password "dbpass" and grants it full access to the "companydb" database.

Explanation:

- Connecting to MariaDB Server: The mysql command is used to connect to the MariaDB server. The -u flag specifies the username (root in this case), and the -p flag prompts for the password.
- Creating a New Database: The CREATE DATABASE SQL command is used to create a new database named "companydb." This database will be used to store data for the new project.
- Creating a New User: The CREATE USER SQL command is used to create a new database user named "dbuser" with the specified password. The GRANT command assigns all privileges on the "companydb" database to the new user. Finally, FLUSH PRIVILEGES reloads the grant tables in the MariaDB server, ensuring that the privileges are applied immediately.

Question 33: System Monitoring

Utilize tools such as top and free to monitor CPU and memory usage. Develop a script that automatically retrieves and displays the following system metrics:

1. CPU Usage:
- Display the current CPU usage percentage.
- Highlight the top processes consuming CPU resources.

2. Memory Usage:
- Display the total memory, used memory, free memory, and available memory.
- Highlight memory-intensive processes.

3. Ensure the script provides real-time monitoring and updates at regular intervals.

Explanation

1. Create a script with the following content:

```bash
#!/bin/bash

# Function to display CPU usage and top processes
function monitor_cpu {
  clear
  echo "***** CPU Usage *****"
  top -bn 1 | grep "Cpu(s)" | sed "s/.*, *\([0-9.]*\)%* id.*/\1/" | awk '{print "CPU Usage: " 100 - $1"%"}'
  echo "Top CPU-consuming processes:"
  top -bn1 | tail -n +8 | head -n 5 | awk '{print $12 ":" $9"%"}'
  sleep 5  # Update every 5 seconds
}
```

```
# Function to display memory usage
function monitor_memory {
  clear
  echo "***** Memory Usage *****"
  free -h
  sleep 5  # Update every 5 seconds
}

# Main function
function main {
  while true; do
    monitor_cpu
    monitor_memory
  done
}

# Execute main function
main
```

Explanation:

- The script consists of two main functions: monitor_cpu and monitor_memory.
- monitor_cpu utilizes the top command to display CPU usage and identify the top CPU-consuming processes.
- monitor_memory uses the free command to display memory usage statistics.
- Both functions clear the terminal screen to provide a clean display.
- The sleep command ensures that the script updates the metrics every 5 seconds.
- The main function continuously calls the monitoring functions in an infinite loop to provide real-time monitoring.

Question 34: Disk Partitioning and Filesystem Management

You have a new disk identified as /dev/sdb on your Linux system.

Tasks:

1. Create Partitions: Partition the disk into two sections of equal size (500MB each).
2. Configure Swap: Prepare the first partition (/dev/sdb1) as swap space for virtual memory usage. Ensure this swap space is automatically activated during system boots.
3. Format Second Partition (XFS): Format the second partition (/dev/sdb2) with the XFS filesystem.

Explanation

1. Partitioning the Disk: Use the fdisk or parted command to create two partitions on the disk /dev/sdb, each with a size of 500MB.
```
$ sudo fdisk /dev/sdb
```
Use the n command to create a new partition, specify the partition size, and repeat the process to create the second partition.

2. Configure Swap: Once the partitions are created, mark the first partition (/dev/sdb1) as swap space.
```
$ sudo mkswap /dev/sdb1
$ sudo swapon /dev/sdb1
```

Add an entry to /etc/fstab to ensure that the swap space is activated during system boots.
```
$ echo "/dev/sdb1  none  swap  defaults  0  0" | sudo tee -a /
```

etc/fstab

3. Format Second Partition (XFS): Format the second partition (/dev/sdb2) with the XFS filesystem.
`$ sudo mkfs.xfs /dev/sdb2`

Optionally, you can mount the XFS partition to a directory:
`$ sudo mkdir /mnt/data`
`$ sudo mount /dev/sdb2 /mnt/data`

Add an entry to /etc/fstab for automatic mounting during system boot:
`$ echo "/dev/sdb2 /mnt/data xfs defaults 0 0" | sudo tee -a /etc/fstab`

Explanation:

- Partitioning: Use fdisk or parted to partition the disk into two equal-sized partitions (/dev/sdb1 and /dev/sdb2).
- Swap Configuration: Create a swap space on /dev/sdb1 using mkswap and activate it with swapon. Then, add an entry to /etc/fstab for automatic activation during system boot.
- Formatting: Format /dev/sdb2 with the XFS filesystem using mkfs.xfs. Optionally, mount it to a directory and add an entry to /etc/fstab for automatic mounting.

Question 35: Logical Volume Management (LVM)

You have two disks available on your Linux system, /dev/sdc and /dev/sdd. You'll prepare them for use with Logical Volume Management (LVM).

Tasks:

1. Initialize Physical Volumes: Prepare both disks (/dev/sdc and /dev/sdd) as physical volumes usable by LVM.
2. Create Volume Group: Group the physical volumes into a volume group named "vg01".
3. Create Logical Volume: Within the volume group "vg01", create a logical volume named "lv01" with a size of 1GB.

Explanation

1. Initialize Physical Volumes: Use the pvcreate command to initialize the disks /dev/sdc and /dev/sdd as physical volumes.
`$ sudo pvcreate /dev/sdc /dev/sdd`

2. Create Volume Group: Once the physical volumes are initialized, create a volume group named "vg01" using the vgcreate command.
`$ sudo vgcreate vg01 /dev/sdc /dev/sdd`
This command groups the physical volumes /dev/sdc and /dev/sdd into the volume group "vg01".

3. Create Logical Volume: Within the volume group "vg01", create a logical volume named "lv01" with a size of 1GB using the lvcreate command.
`$ sudo lvcreate -L 1G -n lv01 vg01`
This command creates a logical volume named "lv01" with a

size of 1GB (-L 1G) within the volume group "vg01".

Explanation:

- Physical Volume Initialization: The pvcreate command prepares the specified disks to be used as physical volumes for LVM.
- Volume Group Creation: The vgcreate command creates a volume group named "vg01" and adds the initialized physical volumes to it.
- Logical Volume Creation: Finally, the lvcreate command creates a logical volume named "lv01" with a specified size within the volume group "vg01".

Question 36: Bash Scripting Challenge

1. Compose a bash script `fmanage` that accomplishes the following tasks:

2. Directory Navigation: Navigate to the user's home directory and list all files and directories.

3. Process Monitoring: Prompt the user for a process name, then continuously monitor and display the CPU and memory usage of that process every 2 seconds until the user terminates the script with Ctrl+C.

4. Conditional Statements: Prompt the user for a file path and check if the file exists at the provided path. Display a message indicating whether the file exists or not.

5. Input Validation: Prompt the user for a filename, check if the file exists and is readable, and display a message based on the file's existence and readability.

Explanation

1. Create a script file `fmanage` with the following content:

```bash
#!/bin/bash

# Directory Navigation
echo "1. Directory Navigation:"
cd ~
ls -la

# Process Monitoring
echo "2. Process Monitoring:"
read -p "Enter the name of the process to monitor: " process_name
while true; do
```

```
  top -b -n 1 | grep "$process_name"
  sleep 2
done

# Conditional Statements
echo "3. Conditional Statements:"
read -p "Enter the path of the file to check: " file_path
if [ -e "$file_path" ]; then
  echo "The file exists."
else
  echo "The file does not exist."
fi

# Input Validation
echo "4. Input Validation:"
read -p "Enter a filename to check: " filename
if [ -e "$filename" ] && [ -r "$filename" ]; then
  echo "The file exists and is readable."
else
  echo "The file does not exist or is not readable."
fi
```

Explanation:

- Directory Navigation: The script navigates to the user's home directory using cd ~ and then lists all files and directories in the home directory with ls -la.
- Process Monitoring: It prompts the user for a process name and enters a loop where it continuously monitors the CPU and memory usage of the specified process every 2 seconds using top -b -n 1 | grep "$process_name" within a while loop.
- Conditional Statements: The script prompts the user for a file path and checks if the file exists at the provided path using the -e flag. It then displays a message indicating whether the file exists or not.
- Input Validation: It prompts the user for a filename and

checks if the file exists and is readable using the -e and -r flags. It displays a message based on the file's existence and readability.

LFCS PRACTICE
EXAM FIVE

Question 1: File Manipulation

You are tasked with performing various file manipulation operations:

1. Content Extraction: You have a compressed file named ~/archive.tar.gz that needs to be extracted to a directory named ~/extracted_data. Ensure successful extraction.
2. File Permissions: Modify the permissions of ~/secure_file.txt to allow read and write access for the owner only, denying access for the group and others. Confirm the permissions have been updated correctly.
3. Text Replacement: Replace all occurrences of the word "apple" with "orange" in ~/fruits.txt. Verify the replacement was successful.

Explanation

1. Content Extraction:

Execute the following command to extract the content of /archive.tar.gz to /extracted_data:
```
$ tar -xzf ~/archive.tar.gz -C ~/extracted_data
```

Confirm the successful extraction by running:
```
$ ls ~/extracted_data
```

2. File Permissions:

Utilize the following command to modify the permissions of /secure_file.txt:
```
$ chmod 600 ~/secure_file.txt
```

Verify the correct permissions using:
`$ ls -l ~/secure_file.txt`

3. Text Replacement:

Use the following command to replace all occurrences of "apple" with "orange" in /fruits.txt:
`$ sed -i 's/apple/orange/g' ~/fruits.txt`

Confirm the successful replacement by examining the file:
`$ cat ~/fruits.txt`

Question 2: Package Management
with Persistence

You are tasked with installing the Vim text editor, ensuring the installation persists through system reboots. Additionally, verify the successful installation and version of the Vim package.

Tasks:

1. Install Vim: Use the package manager to install the Vim text editor.
2. Ensure Persistence: Configure the system to ensure that the Vim installation persists through system reboots.
3. Verify Installation: Confirm the successful installation of Vim and check its version to ensure correctness.

Explanation

1. Install Vim: Use the appropriate package manager to install Vim. The commands may vary depending on your Linux distribution:

For Debian/Ubuntu-based systems:
```
$ sudo apt update
$ sudo apt install vim
```

For CentOS/RHEL-based systems:
```
$ sudo yum install vim
```
For Fedora:
```
$ sudo dnf install vim
```

For openSUSE:
```
$ sudo zypper install vim
```

2. Ensure Persistence: The installation of Vim should automatically persist through system reboots. Modern package managers handle this by default, ensuring that installed packages remain installed after a reboot. However, it's always good to verify this behavior.

3. Verify Installation: After installation, verify the successful installation of Vim and check its version:
`$ vim --version`
This command will display information about the Vim text editor, including its version number.

Explanation:

- Package Installation: Using the appropriate package manager, Vim is installed on the system. The specific commands depend on the Linux distribution being used.
- Persistence: Most modern package managers automatically handle persistence, ensuring that installed packages remain installed even after a system reboot. However, this behavior can be verified to ensure reliability.

Verification: The vim --version command is used to confirm the successful installation of Vim and to check its version number. This ensures that the correct version of Vim is installed and ready for use.

Question 3: Cron Job Management
for System Reporting

You've been tasked with scheduling a cron job to execute a script named daily_report.sh, located in the ~/scripts/ directory, to generate a system report every day at 8:00 PM. The report should include system uptime, disk usage, and currently logged-in users. Set the cron job for the root user and ensure it persists through system reboots.

Tasks:

1. Create the Script: Write a shell script named daily_report.sh that generates the required system report.
2. Schedule the Cron Job: Configure a cron job for the root user to execute the daily_report.sh script daily at 8:00 PM.
3. Ensure Resilience to Reboots: Ensure that the cron job persists through system reboots to continue generating daily reports.

Explanation

1. Create the Script: Create a shell script named daily_report.sh in the ~/scripts/ directory. Open a text editor and enter the following script:

```
#!/bin/bash

# Script to generate daily system report

# Output system uptime
echo "System Uptime:"
uptime
echo ""
```

```
# Output disk usage
echo "Disk Usage:"
df -h
echo ""

# Output currently logged-in users
echo "Currently Logged-In Users:"
who
```

Save the script and make it executable:
```
$ chmod +x ~/scripts/daily_report.sh
```

2. Schedule the Cron Job: Open the crontab file for editing:
```
$ sudo crontab -e
```

Add the following line to schedule the cron job:
```
0 20 * * * /root/scripts/daily_report.sh
```
This cron job will execute the daily_report.sh script every day at 8:00 PM (20:00).

3. Ensure Resilience to Reboots: By default, cron jobs configured in the root user's crontab persist through system reboots. However, it's a good practice to verify this behavior after setting up the cron job.

Explanation:

- Script Creation: A shell script named daily_report.sh is created to generate the required system report. It includes commands to display system uptime, disk usage, and currently logged-in users.
- Cron Job Scheduling: A cron job is scheduled using the crontab -e command for the root user. The job executes the daily_report.sh script every day at 8:00 PM using the appropriate cron timing format (0 20 * * *).

- Resilience to Reboots: Cron jobs configured in the root user's crontab typically persist through system reboots. However, it's important to verify this behavior to ensure that the daily system report continues to be generated reliably.

Question 4: User and Group Management: Adding User to Existing Group

You're tasked with creating a new user named "analyst" and adding this user to an existing group named "data." Ensure that these changes are permanent and persist across system reboots. After completing these actions, confirm that the user has been successfully created and is a member of the correct group.

Tasks:

1. Create the User: Create a new user named "analyst."
2. Add User to Existing Group: Add the user "analyst" to the existing group "data."
3. Ensure Persistence: Ensure that the user and group changes persist across system reboots.
4. Verify User and Group: Confirm that the user "analyst" has been successfully created and is a member of the correct group.

Explanation

1. Create the User: To create the user "analyst," use the useradd command:
$ sudo useradd analyst

2. Add User to Existing Group: To add the user "analyst" to the existing group "data," use the usermod command:
$ sudo usermod -aG data analyst

3. Ensure Persistence: User and group changes made with the useradd and usermod commands typically persist across

system reboots by default. However, it's good practice to verify this persistence after making the changes.

4. Verify User and Group: To verify that the user "analyst" has been successfully created and added to the correct group "data," you can use the following commands:

To check if the user "analyst" exists:
```
$ id analyst
```

To check the groups the user "analyst" belongs to:
```
$ groups analyst
```

Explanation:

- User Creation: The useradd command is used to create a new user named "analyst."
- Group Addition: The usermod command with the -aG option is used to add the user "analyst" to the existing group "data."
- Persistence: User and group changes made with commands like useradd and usermod typically persist across system reboots. However, it's important to verify this to ensure that the changes remain intact.

Verification: The id and groups commands are used to verify that the user "analyst" has been successfully created and added to the correct group "data."

Question 5: System Configuration: Setting Up Custom Welcome Message

You're tasked with setting up a custom system-wide message that displays a welcome message for all users upon login. The message should read: "Welcome to our system, have a great day!" Ensure that this modification is permanent and persists across system reboots.

Tasks:

1. Create or Modify the MOTD file: Add or modify the Message of the Day (MOTD) file to display the custom welcome message.
2. Ensure Persistence: Ensure that the modification to the MOTD file persists across system reboots.

Explanation

1. Create or Modify the MOTD file: The Message of the Day (MOTD) file is typically located in the /etc directory. You can create or modify this file to display the custom welcome message.

```
$ sudo echo "Welcome to our system, have a great day!" > /etc/motd
```

This command overwrites the existing MOTD file with the custom welcome message. If the MOTD file does not exist, this command creates it.

2. Ensure Persistence: Modifications to the MOTD file should persist across system reboots. The motd file is typically read during the login process, so any changes made to it should remain intact.

Explanation:

- MOTD File: The Message of the Day (MOTD) file is a text file that contains a message or information displayed to users upon login. By creating or modifying the MOTD file, you can display a custom welcome message for all users.
- Custom Welcome Message: The custom welcome message "Welcome to our system, have a great day!" is echoed into the MOTD file using the echo command. This command overwrites the existing content of the MOTD file with the custom message.
- Persistence: The MOTD file is typically read during the login process, so any modifications made to it should persist across system reboots. By ensuring that the MOTD file is properly configured, the custom welcome message will continue to be displayed to users every time they log in.

Question 6: Process Management: Listing and Killing Processes

As a system administrator, managing processes is a crucial task. In this scenario, you are required to list all processes owned by a user named "webadmin" and kill the one with the highest RAM usage. Verify your actions.

Tasks:

1. List Processes Owned by User "webadmin": Utilize system utilities to list all processes owned by the user "webadmin".
2. Identify Process with Highest RAM Usage: Analyze the process list to identify the one with the highest RAM usage.
3. Kill Process with Highest RAM Usage: Terminate the process with the highest RAM usage to free up system resources.
4. Verify Actions: Confirm that the process has been successfully terminated and system resources have been released.

Explanation

1. List Processes Owned by User "webadmin": To list all processes owned by the user "webadmin," you can use the ps command with the -u option followed by the username.
`$ ps -u webadmin`
This command displays a list of processes owned by the user "webadmin," along with their details.

2. Identify Process with Highest RAM Usage: To identify the process with the highest RAM usage from the list, you can use the ps command in combination with other utilities like sort and head.
`$ ps -u webadmin --sort=-rss | head -n 2`

This command sorts the processes owned by "webadmin" by their RAM usage (rss field) in descending order and displays the top process with the highest RAM usage.

3. Kill Process with Highest RAM Usage: Once you have identified the process with the highest RAM usage, you can terminate it using the kill command followed by the process ID (PID).

`$ sudo kill <PID>`

Replace <PID> with the process ID of the identified process.

4. Verify Actions: After killing the process, you can verify that it has been successfully terminated by listing processes again or checking system resource usage.

`$ ps -u webadmin`

Additionally, you can monitor system resource usage using tools like top or htop to ensure that the RAM usage has decreased after terminating the process.

Explanation:

- Listing Processes: The ps command is used to list processes on a Linux system. By specifying the -u option followed by the username, you can filter the list to display processes owned by a specific user.
- Identifying Process with Highest RAM Usage: The ps command can sort processes based on various criteria, including RAM usage (rss field). By sorting the list in descending order and displaying the top process using the head command, you can identify the process with the highest RAM usage.
- Killing Process: Once the process with the highest RAM usage is identified, it can be terminated using the kill command followed by the process ID (PID).

Verification: After killing the process, it's essential to verify that it has been successfully terminated. This can be done by listing processes again and checking system resource usage to ensure that the RAM usage has decreased.

Question 7: Storage Management: Partitioning, Formatting, and Mounting

As a system administrator, managing storage is a critical aspect of your role. In this scenario, you are tasked with performing the following tasks:

1. Create a new partition on the disk /dev/sde, assign it the partition number 1, and set its size to 500MB.
2. Format this new partition (/dev/sde1) with the ext4 filesystem.
3. Mount this new partition at the /mnt/mydir directory.
4. Ensure that this new partition is automatically mounted at the same location every time the system boots.

Explanation

1. Create a New Partition: Use a partitioning tool like fdisk or parted to create a new partition on the disk /dev/sde with the desired size.
`$ sudo fdisk /dev/sde`

Follow the prompts to create a new partition (e.g., using the n command) and set its size to 500MB.

2. Format the New Partition: Once the partition is created, format it with the ext4 filesystem using the mkfs command.
`$ sudo mkfs.ext4 /dev/sde1`
This command creates an ext4 filesystem on the partition /dev/sde1.

3. Mount the New Partition: Create a mount point at /mnt/mydir if it doesn't exist already and mount the new partition

to this directory.
```
$ sudo mkdir -p /mnt/mydir
$ sudo mount /dev/sde1 /mnt/mydir
```
This mounts the partition /dev/sde1 to the directory /mnt/mydir.

4. Ensure Automatic Mounting: To ensure that the new partition is automatically mounted at the same location every time the system boots, add an entry to the /etc/fstab file.

Open /etc/fstab in a text editor and add the following line:
```
/dev/sde1 /mnt/mydir ext4 defaults 0 0
```
This entry specifies that the partition /dev/sde1 should be mounted at /mnt/mydir with the ext4 filesystem using default options (defaults). The 0 0 at the end specifies options for filesystem checks.

Explanation:

- Partition Creation: Using a partitioning tool like fdisk or parted, you can create a new partition on the specified disk (/dev/sde) and set its size to 500MB.
- Formatting: After creating the partition, format it with the ext4 filesystem using the mkfs.ext4 command.
- Mounting: Create a directory (/mnt/mydir) as the mount point and mount the new partition to this directory using the mount command.
- Automatic Mounting: To ensure that the partition is automatically mounted at the same location every time the system boots, add an entry to the /etc/fstab file specifying the partition, mount point, filesystem type, and options.

Question 8: Archives
and Compression

As a system administrator, managing logs and backups is critical for maintaining system integrity. In this scenario, you are tasked with the following operations:

1. Create a tar archive (/tmp/log_archive.tar) of the entire /var/ log directory.
2. Compress this tar archive using gzip.
3. Move the compressed archive to the /backup_logs directory.
4. Verify that the archive has been successfully moved to the / backup_logs directory.
5. Schedule a cron job to perform this task every Monday at 3 a.m.

Explanation

1. Create Tar Archive: Use the tar command to create a tar archive of the /var/log directory.
`$ sudo tar -cvf /tmp/log_archive.tar /var/log`
This command creates a tar archive named log_archive.tar of the /var/log directory and saves it in the /tmp directory.

2. Compress the Archive: Use the gzip command to compress the tar archive.
`$ sudo gzip /tmp/log_archive.tar`
This command compresses the tar archive log_archive.tar using gzip, resulting in log_archive.tar.gz.

3. Move the Compressed Archive: Move the compressed archive to the /backup_logs directory.
`$ sudo mv /tmp/log_archive.tar.gz /backup_logs/`
This   command   moves   the   compressed   archive

log_archive.tar.gz to the /backup_logs directory.

4. Verify Archive Move: Verify that the archive has been successfully moved to the /backup_logs directory.
`$ ls /backup_logs/log_archive.tar.gz`
This command lists the contents of the /backup_logs directory, confirming the presence of the compressed archive.

5. Schedule Cron Job: Schedule a cron job to perform this task every Monday at 3 a.m. Open the crontab file using crontab -e and add the following line:
`0 3 * * 1 sudo tar -cvf /tmp/log_archive.tar /var/log && sudo gzip /tmp/log_archive.tar && sudo mv /tmp/log_archive.tar.gz /backup_logs/`
This cron job will execute the specified commands (creating tar archive, compressing it, and moving to backup directory) every Monday at 3 a.m.

Explanation:

- Creating Tar Archive: Tar (tar) is used to create archives. Here, we create a tar archive of the /var/log directory.
- Compressing Archive: The gzip command is used to compress the tar archive into a gzip-compressed file (tar.gz).
- Moving Archive: The mv command moves the compressed archive to the specified directory (/backup_logs).
- Verifying Move: We use ls to confirm that the compressed archive exists in the /backup_logs directory.
- Scheduling Cron Job: A cron job is scheduled using crontab -e, specifying the desired frequency (every Monday at 3 a.m.) and the commands to execute.

Question 9: Advanced File Operations

As a system administrator, understanding how to efficiently search for and manage files is essential. In this scenario, you are tasked with using the find command to locate and list all files in the /etc directory that were modified within the last 72 hours. The output should be formatted to include file permissions, number of links, owner, group, size in bytes, and modification time in a human-readable format.

Explanation

To accomplish the task, run:

```
$ find /etc -type f -mtime -3 -exec ls -l --time-style=long-iso {} +
```

Explanation:

 # find /etc -type f: This command starts the find operation in the /etc directory and searches only for regular files (-type f).
 # -mtime -3: This parameter specifies that we want to find files modified within the last 72 hours (-mtime -3). # The -mtime option is used to specify the modification time of the file. The value -3 means within the last three days.
 # -exec ls -l --time-style=long-iso {} +: This part of the command executes the ls command on the found files. The # ls -l option lists files in long format, including permissions, number of links, owner, group, size, and modification time. The --time-style=long-iso option ensures that the modification time is displayed in a human-readable format.
 # {} and +: These symbols are placeholders for the found files. {} represents the list of found files, and + indicates that ls should be executed on as many files as possible at once, which improves efficiency.

Question 10: Advanced Kernel and Package Management

As a system administrator, maintaining an up-to-date kernel and packages is crucial for security and performance. In this scenario, you are tasked with updating the current kernel version to the latest stable release available in the repository and then updating all the packages on the system. Finally, you need to verify the successful update of the kernel and packages.

Explanation

1. Update Kernel:

To update the kernel to the latest stable release, follow these steps:
```
$ sudo apt update
$ sudo apt install linux-generic
```
This command updates the kernel to the latest stable version available in the repository.

2. Update Packages:

To update all packages on the system, execute the following command:
```
$ sudo apt upgrade
```
This command upgrades all installed packages to their latest versions.

3. Verify Update:

After completing the updates, you can verify the kernel and package versions using the following commands:

4. Check Kernel Version:

`$ uname -r`

This command displays the currently running kernel version.

5. Check Package Updates:

`$ sudo apt list --upgradable`

This command lists all packages that have available upgrades.

6. Check Package Version:

`$ dpkg -l | grep '^ii'`

This command lists all installed packages along with their versions.

Explanation:

- Updating Kernel: The linux-generic package ensures that you have the latest stable kernel version installed on your system. By running apt install linux-generic, the package manager fetches the latest available kernel version from the repository and installs it.

- Updating Packages: The apt upgrade command upgrades all installed packages to their latest available versions. It updates packages while also resolving dependencies and ensuring system stability.

- Verification: After updating, verifying the kernel version and available package updates ensures that the updates were successful. The uname -r command displays the kernel version, while apt list --upgradable lists available package upgrades. The dpkg -l | grep '^ii' command lists all installed packages along with their versions.

Question 11: Advanced Networking

As a system administrator, you are tasked with configuring a static IP address (192.168.1.101) for the network interface eth2. You need to ensure that the network configuration persists across reboots.

Explanation

1. Identify Network Configuration Files:

Determine the appropriate network configuration file for your distribution. Common locations include /etc/network/ interfaces for Debian-based systems and /etc/sysconfig/ network-scripts/ifcfg-ethX for Red Hat-based systems.

2. Edit Network Configuration File:

Open the network configuration file using a text editor such as nano or vim. Add or modify the configuration for eth2 to include the desired static IP address.

For Debian-based systems (e.g., Ubuntu), edit /etc/network/ interfaces:

```
auto eth2
iface eth2 inet static
    address 192.168.1.101
    netmask 255.255.255.0
    gateway 192.168.1.1
```

For Red Hat-based systems (e.g., CentOS), edit /etc/sysconfig/ network-scripts/ifcfg-eth2:

```
DEVICE=eth2
BOOTPROTO=none
ONBOOT=yes
IPADDR=192.168.1.101
NETMASK=255.255.255.0
```

You can replace 192.168.1.101 with the desired static IP address and adjust other parameters as necessary (e.g., netmask, gateway).

3. Restart Networking Service:

After saving the changes, restart the networking service to apply the new configuration:

```
$ sudo systemctl restart networking     # For Debian-based
systems
$ sudo systemctl restart network         # For Red Hat-based
systems
```

This command reloads the network configuration, applying the changes to the eth2 interface.

4. Verify Configuration:

Verify that the static IP address configuration is applied correctly using the following command:

```
$ ip addr show eth2
```

This command displays the IP address configuration for the eth2 interface. Ensure that the configured IP address, netmask, and gateway match the settings you specified.

5. Persistence Across Reboots:

The changes made to the network configuration file will persist across reboots, ensuring that the static IP address for eth2 remains configured even after a system restart.

Explanation:

Configuring a static IP address involves modifying the network configuration file for the respective network interface. The configuration typically includes parameters such as the IP address, netmask, and gateway. Editing the appropriate network configuration file and restarting the networking service ensures that the changes take effect. Verifying the configuration with the ip addr show command confirms that the static IP address is correctly configured. By default, network configuration changes made to the network configuration file persist across reboots, ensuring that the static IP address configuration remains intact.

Question 12: Advanced
Storage Management

As a system administrator, you are tasked with resizing the logical volume named lv01 in the volume group vg01 to increase its size by 100MB. Additionally, you need to ensure that the filesystem within the logical volume is resized to utilize the additional space. Verify that the resizing operation was successful and that the filesystem can utilize the additional space.

Explanation

1. Identify Available Space:

Before resizing, check the available space in the volume group to ensure sufficient free space exists to extend the logical volume.
$ sudo vgdisplay vg01

2. Resize Logical Volume:

Use the lvresize command to increase the size of the logical volume by 100MB.
$ sudo lvresize -L +100M /dev/vg01/lv01
This command increases the size of lv01 by 100MB. Adjust the size as needed based on your requirements.

3. Resize Filesystem:

If the logical volume contains a filesystem (e.g., ext4, xfs), resize the filesystem to utilize the additional space.

For ext4 filesystems:

```
$ sudo resize2fs /dev/vg01/lv01
```

For xfs filesystems:
```
$ sudo xfs_growfs /dev/vg01/lv01
```

4. Verify Resizing:

Verify that the resizing operation was successful and that the filesystem can utilize the additional space.
```
$ df -h
```
This command displays the filesystem usage. Ensure that the filesystem size reflects the increase in space.

Explanation:

Resizing a logical volume involves increasing its size within the volume group and then resizing the filesystem to utilize the additional space. The lvresize command is used to modify the size of the logical volume, while tools like resize2fs (for ext4 filesystems) or xfs_growfs (for xfs filesystems) are used to resize the filesystem to match the new size of the logical volume. Verifying the resizing operation ensures that the filesystem can indeed utilize the additional space.

Question 13: Implementing Firewall Rules to Enhance Network Security

As a system administrator following a distribution-agnostic approach, you are responsible for bolstering network security by implementing firewall rules. Your current task involves creating a persistent firewall rule to block all incoming traffic on UDP port 123. Develop a solution that ensures the rule persists across system reboots, considering the distribution-agnostic nature of your approach.

Explanation

1. Identify the Current Firewall Configuration: Before implementing any changes, it's essential to understand the current firewall configuration to ensure compatibility and prevent unintended consequences.

2. Create a Rule to Block Incoming UDP Traffic on Port 123: We'll use the iptables command to create a rule specifically blocking UDP traffic on port 123. This rule should be designed to persist across system reboots.

```
$ sudo iptables -A INPUT -p udp --dport 123 -j DROP
```

sudo: Executes the command with superuser privileges.
-A INPUT: Appends the rule to the INPUT chain, which handles incoming traffic.
-p udp: Specifies the protocol as UDP.
--dport 123: Indicates the destination port as 123.
-j DROP: Instructs iptables to drop (i.e., block) matching packets.

3. Save the Firewall Rules: To ensure that the rule persists

across reboots, we need to save the current iptables configuration.

`$ sudo iptables-save > /etc/iptables/rules.v4`

This command saves the current iptables configuration to the specified file (rules.v4 in the /etc/iptables/ directory). On some distributions, the path may vary, but it typically resides within /etc/iptables/ or /etc/sysconfig/.

4. Reload the Firewall Configuration During Boot: We'll configure the system to reload the saved iptables configuration during boot.

Systemd Approach: For systems using systemd, create a systemd service unit to reload the firewall rules during boot.

- Create a service unit file (e.g., iptables-restore.service) in the /etc/systemd/system/ directory.

- Add appropriate directives to specify dependencies and actions (e.g., ExecStart) for reloading the iptables rules.

- Enable the service to ensure it starts automatically on boot:

`$ sudo systemctl enable iptables-restore.service`

SysVinit Approach: For systems using SysVinit, add a script to reload the iptables rules in the appropriate runlevel directories (e.g., /etc/rc.d/).

5. Testing: After implementing the rule and configuring its persistence, it's crucial to test the firewall to verify that the desired behavior is achieved. Test by attempting to establish UDP connections on port 123 from external sources.

Question 14: Implementing Log Rotation Strategies for System Maintenance

As a system administrator adhering to a distribution-agnostic approach, you're tasked with ensuring the efficient management of system logs to prevent disk space issues. Your objective is to implement a log rotation strategy using logrotate. Configure logrotate to compress and rotate /var/log/syslog logs on a daily basis, while retaining rotated logs for 14 days before discarding them. Develop a comprehensive solution that addresses these requirements, considering the distribution-agnostic nature of your approach.

Explanation

1. Identify Log Files to Rotate: Before configuring log rotation, it's essential to identify the log files that need to be rotated. This typically includes system logs, application logs, and any other logs that accumulate over time.

2. Install logrotate if Not Already Installed: Although logrotate is commonly installed by default on most Linux distributions, ensure that it's installed on the system. Use the appropriate package manager for the distribution being used:

# For Debian/Ubuntu-based distributions
$ sudo apt-get install logrotate

# For Red Hat/CentOS-based distributions
$ sudo yum install logrotate

3. Configure Log Rotation with logrotate: Edit the logrotate configuration file (/etc/logrotate.conf or /etc/logrotate.d/*) to

define the log rotation strategy. If necessary, create a new configuration file for specific logs.
`$ sudo nano /etc/logrotate.d/my_logs`

Add the following configuration to rotate logs daily, compress them, and retain rotated logs for 14 days:

```
/var/log/syslog {
  daily
  rotate 14
  compress
  delaycompress
  missingok
  notifempty
}
```

daily: Specifies that log rotation should occur daily.
rotate 14: Indicates that rotated logs should be kept for 14 days before being discarded.
compress: Directs logrotate to compress rotated logs using gzip.
delaycompress: Delays compression of rotated logs until the next rotation cycle to ensure compatibility with certain applications.
missingok: Ignores errors if the log file is missing.
notifempty: Skips rotation if the log file is empty.

4. Verify Logrotate Configuration: Before proceeding, verify the syntax and effectiveness of the logrotate configuration using the --debug option:
`$ sudo logrotate --debug /etc/logrotate.conf`
This command checks the configuration for errors and provides detailed information about the rotation process.

5. Testing: After configuring logrotate, monitor the log files and observe the rotation process to ensure that it functions

as expected. Check disk usage periodically to confirm that log files are being rotated and compressed appropriately.

Question 15: Advanced System Troubleshooting and Optimization

As a system administrator committed to a distribution-agnostic approach, you encounter two complex system issues demanding immediate attention:

Part 1: High CPU Usage Your system exhibits sluggishness, prompting investigation revealing high CPU consumption. Your task involves identifying the process(es) responsible for this elevated CPU usage. Once identified, determine the root cause of the excessive CPU consumption and propose solutions to mitigate the issue.

Part 2: Intermittent Network Connectivity Multiple users report intermittent network connectivity issues, disrupting their workflow. Your responsibility is to investigate the underlying cause of these connectivity problems and propose effective solutions to ensure consistent and reliable network access for all users.

Develop a comprehensive solution addressing both parts of the problem, considering the distribution-agnostic nature of your troubleshooting approach.

Explanation

Part 1: High CPU Usage

1. Identify High CPU Processes: Utilize system monitoring tools such as top, htop, or atop to identify processes consuming excessive CPU resources. Sort processes by CPU usage to pinpoint the culprit(s).

2. Investigate Root Cause: Once identified, delve deeper into the offending process(es) to determine the root cause of the high CPU consumption. Common causes include:

- Misbehaving applications or services.
- Infinite loops or excessive resource utilization within scripts.
- Resource contention due to improper configuration or insufficient hardware resources.

3. Mitigation Solutions: Based on the root cause analysis, implement appropriate mitigation strategies:

- Optimize Code or Configuration: Work with developers to optimize resource-intensive applications or scripts, fixing performance bottlenecks.
- Resource Allocation: Adjust resource limits for processes using tools like nice, renice, or ulimit to prioritize critical tasks and prevent resource starvation.
- Hardware Upgrades: If hardware constraints are the issue, consider upgrading CPU, memory, or storage to better accommodate system demands.

Part 2: Intermittent Network Connectivity

1. Gather Network Information: Collect network-related data using tools like ifconfig, ip, netstat, or iptraf to assess network interfaces, routing tables, and network statistics.

2. Identify Connectivity Issues: Analyze logs and conduct tests (e.g., ping, traceroute) to pinpoint the nature and scope of connectivity issues:

- Check for packet loss, latency spikes, or network congestion.
- Investigate DNS resolution problems or DHCP lease issues.
- Examine firewall rules, network device configurations, and switch/router status.

3. Implement Solutions: Based on the identified issues, implement appropriate solutions to ensure consistent network access:

- Network Configuration Review: Verify network interface configurations, DNS settings, and routing tables for accuracy.
- Firewall and Security Configuration: Review firewall rules and security policies to ensure they're not blocking legitimate traffic.
- Network Device Troubleshooting: Check network device configurations, update firmware, and inspect hardware for faults.
- Traffic Management: Implement Quality of Service (QoS) policies to prioritize critical traffic and mitigate network congestion.

Question 16: Container Management with Podman

As a system administrator adhering to a distribution-agnostic approach, you're tasked with configuring and managing containers using Podman. Follow the steps below to complete the task:

1. Install Podman on your system.
2. Pull the official CentOS image from the Docker registry.
3. Create and run a CentOS container named "centos_server."
4. Configure the container to restart automatically unless manually stopped.
5. Verify the successful creation and running of the container.

Explanation

1. Installing Podman: Ensure Podman is installed on the system. Podman is a daemonless container engine for managing containers, pods, and container images.

```
# Installation on Debian/Ubuntu-based distributions
$ sudo apt-get install -y podman
```

```
# Installation on Red Hat/CentOS-based distributions
$ sudo yum install -y podman
```

2. Pulling the Official CentOS Image: Pull the official CentOS image from the Docker registry using Podman.
```
$ podman pull docker.io/library/centos:latest
```
This command retrieves the latest CentOS image from the Docker registry.

3. Creating and Running a CentOS Container: Create and run

a CentOS container named "centos_server" from the pulled image.

```
$ podman run -d --name centos_server docker.io/library/centos:latest
```

-d: Detached mode, which runs the container in the background.
--name centos_server: Specifies the name of the container as "centos_server."

4. Configuring Automatic Restart: Ensure that the container restarts automatically unless manually stopped. We can achieve this by adding the --restart=always option.

```
$ podman run -d --name centos_server --restart=always docker.io/library/centos:latest
```

With --restart=always, the container will restart automatically whenever it exits, unless explicitly stopped.

5. Verifying Container Creation and Running: Verify that the container "centos_server" is successfully created and running.

```
$ podman ps -a
```

This command lists all containers, including those that are stopped (-a option). Ensure that the "centos_server" container is in the list and has the status "Up" if it's running.

Question 17: Network Troubleshooting: DNS Resolution Issues

As a system administrator adhering to a distribution-agnostic approach, you encounter DNS resolution issues on your system. Your task is to diagnose and rectify these issues thoroughly. This involves inspecting the DNS configuration, validating DNS resolution using appropriate utilities, and implementing any necessary adjustments to the DNS settings to ensure persistence across system reboots. Develop a comprehensive solution addressing these requirements while considering the distribution-agnostic nature of your approach.

Explanation

1. Inspecting DNS Configuration: Begin by examining the DNS configuration settings to identify any potential misconfigurations or inconsistencies.

```
# View DNS resolver configuration
$ cat /etc/resolv.conf
```

```
# Check DNS server settings
$ nmcli dev show | grep 'IP4.DNS'
```

Ensure that the DNS servers listed in /etc/resolv.conf or obtained from NetworkManager (nmcli) are correct and accessible.

2. Validating DNS Resolution: Verify DNS resolution using appropriate utilities like nslookup, dig, or host. Test both domain names and IP addresses to ensure proper

functionality.

```
# Test DNS resolution for a domain name
$ nslookup example.com
```

```
# Test reverse DNS resolution for an IP address
$ dig -x 8.8.8.8
```

```
# Verify DNS resolution using host command
$ host example.com
```

Ensure that DNS queries return valid results without errors or timeouts, indicating successful resolution.

3. Implementing Adjustments to DNS Settings: If DNS resolution issues persist, implement necessary adjustments to the DNS settings:

- Update DNS Servers: If incorrect or inaccessible DNS servers are detected, update the DNS server settings either manually or through network configuration tools like NetworkManager (nmcli) or systemd-resolved.
- Configure DNS Search Domains: Add or update DNS search domains in /etc/resolv.conf or network configuration files (/etc/sysconfig/network-scripts/ifcfg-* for Red Hat/CentOS, / etc/network/interfaces for Debian/Ubuntu) to ensure proper domain name resolution.
- Flush DNS Cache: Clear the DNS cache to remove any stale or incorrect entries that might be causing resolution issues.
- Check Firewall Settings: Ensure that DNS traffic is allowed through the firewall by inspecting firewall rules (iptables, firewalld) and adjusting them if necessary.

4. Ensuring Persistence Across System Reboots: To ensure that DNS settings persist across system reboots, make the necessary changes in configuration files or use network

configuration tools that support persistence:
- Update /etc/resolv.conf or network configuration files with the correct DNS settings.
- For NetworkManager-based systems, use nmcli to update DNS settings and ensure they are saved.
- On systemd-based systems, ensure that changes made through systemd-resolved or resolved.conf are persistent.

5. Testing and Verification: After implementing adjustments, retest DNS resolution to confirm that the issues have been resolved:
```
$ nslookup example.com
```
Verify that DNS queries return accurate results without errors, indicating successful resolution.

Question 18: Database Management

You have a Linux system with PostgreSQL installed. Connect to the PostgreSQL server using the default "postgres" user and perform the following tasks:

1. Create a new database named "salesdb."
2. Establish a new user "salesuser" with the password "salespass" and grant them full access to the "salesdb" database.
3. Ensure that these database and user creation changes persist through system reboots.

Explanation

1. Connect to PostgreSQL:

Log in to the PostgreSQL server using the default "postgres" user. You can do this via the command-line interface:
$ sudo -i -u postgres
This command switches the current user to "postgres" and gives you access to PostgreSQL.

2. Create a New Database:

Once connected to PostgreSQL, create a new database named "salesdb" using the createdb command:
$ createdb salesdb
This command will create a new PostgreSQL database named "salesdb."

3. Establish a New User:

After creating the database, establish a new user "salesuser" with the password "salespass." Use the createuser command to achieve this:

`$ createuser salesuser --password`

You will be prompted to enter the password for the new user "salesuser." Enter "salespass" when prompted.

4. Grant User Access to the Database:

Grant the new user "salesuser" full access to the "salesdb" database. You can do this using the psql command-line utility:

`$ psql -c "GRANT ALL PRIVILEGES ON DATABASE salesdb TO salesuser;"`

This command grants all privileges on the "salesdb" database to the user "salesuser," allowing them full access.

5. Ensure Persistence Across Reboots:

To ensure that the changes made to the PostgreSQL database and user persist through system reboots, you need to modify the PostgreSQL configuration file.

First, locate the PostgreSQL configuration file. It is commonly named postgresql.conf and is located in the PostgreSQL data directory, which varies depending on the installation method and distribution. A typical location is /etc/postgresql/<version>/main/postgresql.conf.

Edit the configuration file using a text editor such as nano or vim:

`$ sudo nano /etc/postgresql/<version>/main/postgresql.conf`

Find the line containing listen_addresses and ensure it is set to localhost to only allow local connections. This enhances security by restricting remote access to the PostgreSQL server.

Next, ensure that the PostgreSQL service starts automatically on system boot. This can be achieved by enabling the PostgreSQL service:

```
$ sudo systemctl enable postgresql
```

Finally, restart the PostgreSQL service to apply the changes:

```
$ sudo systemctl restart postgresql
```

Now, the changes made to the database and user configuration will persist through system reboots.

Question 19: System Monitoring and Process Management

Suppose you have a critical task named "myapp" running on your system. Your objective is to elevate its priority to -5. Confirm that the adjustment is effective and enduring across system reboots.

Explanation

1. Identify Process ID (PID):

First, you need to identify the PID of the "myapp" process.
`$ ps aux | grep myapp`
Note down the PID associated with the "myapp" process.

2. Elevate Process Priority:

Once you have the PID, use the renice command to adjust the priority of the process to -5.
`$ sudo renice -n -5 -p <PID>`
Replace <PID> with the actual PID of the "myapp" process.

3. Verify Priority Adjustment:

After adjusting the priority, verify that the change is effective.
`$ ps -o pid,ni,cmd -p <PID>`
This command displays the PID, nice value (priority), and command associated with the specified PID. Ensure that the nice value for the "myapp" process is now -5.

4. Ensure Persistence Across Reboots:

To ensure that the priority adjustment persists across system reboots, you can create a systemd service unit to set the priority during system startup.

Create a systemd service unit file, such as myapp_priority.service, in the /etc/systemd/system/ directory:

```
[Unit]
Description=Adjust priority for myapp

[Service]
ExecStart=/usr/bin/renice -n -5 -p <PID>

[Install]
WantedBy=multi-user.target
```

Replace <PID> with the PID of the "myapp" process.

Enable the service to start at boot:
```
$ sudo systemctl enable myapp_priority.service
```
This ensures that the priority adjustment is applied every time the system boots.

Explanation:

Elevating the priority of a critical task such as "myapp" can ensure that it receives more CPU time, improving its responsiveness and reducing potential delays. The renice command is used to adjust the priority of a running process, and verifying the adjustment ensures its effectiveness. Creating a systemd service unit to apply the priority adjustment at boot ensures that the change persists across system reboots.

Question 20: Special Permissions and Sticky Bit Configuration

Given a directory named /var/sticky/ on your Linux system, your objectives are as follows:

1. Apply the sticky bit special permission to the /var/sticky/ directory.
2. Confirm the successful application of the sticky bit.
3. Ensure that the sticky bit permission remains effective even after system reboots.
4. Verify the existence of the directory and its current permissions before and after the modification.

Explanation

1. Verify the Existence of the Directory:

First, check if the directory /var/sticky/ exists. Use the following command:
`$ ls -ld /var/sticky/`

If the directory does not exist, create it with:
`$ sudo mkdir -p /var/sticky/`

2. Check Current Permissions:

Before applying any changes, verify the current permissions of the directory:
`$ ls -ld /var/sticky/`

This command will output something like:
drwxr-xr-x 2 root root 4096 May 16 14:00 /var/sticky/

3. Apply the Sticky Bit:

To apply the sticky bit, use the chmod command:
`$ sudo chmod +t /var/sticky/`

The sticky bit can also be set using the numeric mode:
`$ sudo chmod 1777 /var/sticky/`

4. Confirm the Application of the Sticky Bit:

Verify that the sticky bit has been applied correctly by listing the directory's details again:
`$ ls -ld /var/sticky/`

The output should now include a t at the end of the permissions string:
`drwxrwxrwt 2 root root 4096 May 16 14:00 /var/sticky/`
The t indicates that the sticky bit is set.

Question 21: Network Configuration and Management

You are tasked with SSHing into a remote server named server01 using the username Amr and a provided password system. Upon successful login, execute the following operations:

1. Add an Additional DNS Resolver: Add a DNS resolver (nameserver) to this system with the IP address 8.8.8.8.
2. Incorporate a Static Host Entry: Add a static host entry so that the hostname database resolves to the IP address 192.168.69.34.
3. Identify the IP Address of the eth1 Network Interface: Determine the IP address assigned to the eth1 network interface on server01.
4. Introduce a Temporary Static Route: Introduce a temporary static route to direct network traffic intended for the 192.168.69.0/24 network via the IP address of eth1.
5. Verify Changes: Verify that each change has been successfully implemented.

Explanation

1. SSH into the Remote Server:

Open your terminal and use the ssh command to log into server01:
`$ ssh Amr@server01`
When prompted, enter the password system.

2. Add an Additional DNS Resolver:

Edit the resolv.conf file in the /etc/ directory to add the new

DNS resolver:
```
$ sudo vim /etc/resolv.conf
```

Add the following line to the file:
```
nameserver 8.8.8.8
```

Save and exit the editor (for nano, press Ctrl+X, then Y, and Enter).

Verification:
```
$ cat /etc/resolv.conf
```

Ensure the output includes:
```
nameserver 8.8.8.8
```

3. Incorporate a Static Host Entry:

Edit the hosts file to add the static host entry:
```
$ sudo vim /etc/hosts
```

Add the following line to the file:
```
192.168.69.34 database
```

Save and exit the editor.

Verification:
```
$ cat /etc/hosts
```

Ensure the output includes:
```
192.168.69.34 database
```

4. Identify the IP Address of the eth1 Network Interface:

Use the ip or ifconfig command to identify the IP address of eth1:
```
$ ip addr show eth1
```

Look for the inet line in the output, which will display the IP address. Suppose the IP address is 192.168.1.100.

Verification:
`$ ip addr show eth1 | grep inet`
Confirm the IP address is correctly identified.

5. Introduce a Temporary Static Route:

Add a static route to direct traffic for the 192.168.69.0/24 network via the eth1 IP address (192.168.1.100):
`$ sudo ip route add 192.168.69.0/24 via 192.168.1.100`

Verification:
`$ ip route`

Ensure the route is listed in the routing table:
`192.168.69.0/24 via 192.168.1.100 dev eth1`

Question 22: System Recovery and Root Password Management

As a system administrator, you're tasked with the following duties:

1. Booting into Emergency Mode and Recovering Root Password: Boot your system into emergency mode and recover the root password.
2. Changing the Root Password: Change the root password to secure_password.

Explanation

1. Booting into Emergency Mode: Emergency mode is a minimal environment where only essential services are started. To boot into emergency mode, you'll need to interrupt the boot process and edit the boot parameters. The exact method can vary depending on the boot loader used (GRUB, systemd-boot, etc.). Here's how you can do it with GRUB:

2. Reboot your system.

When the GRUB menu appears, use the arrow keys to select the kernel you want to boot and press the "e" key to edit its parameters.

3. Find the line that starts with linux or linuxefi and contains the kernel parameters. Add emergency or systemd.unit=emergency.target at the end of this line.

4. Press Ctrl + X or F10 to boot with the modified parameters.

Your system should now boot into emergency mode.

2. Recovering the Root Password: In emergency mode, the root file system is mounted in read-only mode, so you'll need to remount it in read-write mode to change the password. Use the following commands:
`$ mount -o remount,rw /`

Now, you can use the passwd command to change the root password:
`$ passwd`

Follow the prompts to enter and confirm the new password (secure_password in this case).

3. Changing the Root Password: If you've successfully recovered the root password and are logged in as root, you can change the password directly using the passwd command:
`$ passwd`

Follow the prompts to enter and confirm the new password (secure_password).

4. Rebooting the System: After changing the root password, you can reboot the system to ensure that the changes take effect:
`$ reboot`

Your system will now boot normally with the new root password.

Question 23: Troubleshooting
Complex System Issues

As a system administrator, you're tasked with resolving two distinct issues:

1. Identify and resolve issues related to slow disk performance on the /dev/sdb disk drive.
2. Troubleshoot and fix issues with hostname resolution preventing access to remote servers.

Explanation

1. Identifying and Resolving Disk Performance Issues:

Monitor Disk I/O Statistics: Use the iostat command to monitor disk I/O statistics:
```
$ iostat -d -x /dev/sdb
```

If the %iowait value is high, it suggests a potential bottleneck.

Measure Disk Read Speed: Use the hdparm command to measure disk read speed:
```
$ sudo hdparm -Tt /dev/sdb
```

If the speed is significantly lower than expected, it could indicate a hardware issue.

Check for File System Errors: Run a file system check to identify and repair errors:
```
$ sudo umount /dev/sdb   # Ensure the drive is unmounted
$ sudo fsck /dev/sdb
```

Defragmentation (Optional): Consider defragmenting the

drive if heavily fragmented. However, this is typically unnecessary for ext4 and XFS file systems.

2. Troubleshooting Hostname Resolution Issues:

Check Network Connectivity: Use the ping command to check network connectivity to the remote server:
$ ping -c 4 remote_server_ip

If the ping fails, investigate network connectivity issues.

Verify DNS Resolution: Use nslookup or dig to check DNS resolution of the hostname:
$ nslookup remote_server_hostname

If the hostname does not resolve to an IP address, there might be a DNS issue.

Check Hosts and Resolv.conf Files: Inspect the hosts and resolv.conf files in the /etc/ directory for incorrect entries:
$ cat /etc/hosts
$ cat /etc/resolv.conf

Change DNS Server: If the DNS server is unresponsive, consider switching to a different DNS server, such as Google's public DNS:
$ sudo nano /etc/resolv.conf

Edit the file to include Google's DNS servers:
nameserver 8.8.8.8
nameserver 8.8.4.4

Question 24: Implementing
Firewall Rules to Deny Incoming
Traffic on TCP Port 22

As a system administrator, you're tasked with implementing a firewall rule to deny incoming traffic on TCP port 22. Ensure that the rule persists across system reboots.

Explanation

1. Identify the Firewall Management Tool: Linux distributions use various firewall management tools, such as iptables, firewalld, or ufw. Determine which tool is being used on your system before proceeding.

2. Implement the Firewall Rule: Once you've identified the firewall management tool, you can create a rule to deny incoming traffic on TCP port 22. Below are instructions for different firewall management tools:

Using iptables:
```
$ sudo iptables -A INPUT -p tcp --dport 22 -j DROP
```

Using firewalld:
```
$ sudo firewall-cmd --zone=public --add-rich-rule='rule family="ipv4" source address="0.0.0.0/0" port port=22 protocol=tcp reject'
```

Using ufw:
```
$ sudo ufw deny 22/tcp
```

3. Persist the Firewall Rule: To ensure that the firewall rule persists across system reboots, you need to save the firewall configuration. Here's how to do it for each firewall

management tool:

iptables: You can use the iptables-save command to save the current firewall rules to a file. The exact method of restoring these rules on boot may vary depending on your distribution. Consult your distribution's documentation for specific instructions.
firewalld: Firewalld automatically persists firewall rules. Once you've added the rule, it will be saved and loaded on system boot.
ufw: Ufw automatically persists firewall rules. Once you've added the rule, it will be saved and loaded on system boot.

4. Verify the Firewall Rule: After implementing and persisting the firewall rule, verify that it is active and working as expected. You can use the following commands to check:

iptables:
```
$ sudo iptables -L INPUT
```

firewalld:
```
$ sudo firewall-cmd --list-all
```

ufw:
```
$ sudo ufw status
```

These commands will display the current firewall configuration, including the rule to deny incoming traffic on TCP port 22.

Question 25: File and
Directory Permissions

In a Linux environment, configure the /tmp directory such that it has the sticky bit set. This means that only the owner of a file can delete or rename the file within this directory.

Explanation

Set the sticky bit for the /tmp directory
`$ chmod +t /tmp`
This command sets the sticky bit for the /tmp directory.

Explanation:

When the sticky bit is set on a directory, only the owner of a file can delete or rename the file. Other users, even if they have write permissions on the directory, cannot delete or rename files owned by others. This is particularly useful for directories like /tmp, which are world-writable and can be used by multiple users.

Question 26: File Permissions

In a Linux environment, configure the system so that all new files created in the current directory have the default permissions -rw-r-----. This means that the owner has read and write permissions, the group has read permissions, and others have no permissions.

Explanation

The umask command can be used to set the default permissions for new files.
The umask value is subtracted from the full permissions (666 for files and 777 for directories) to get the default permissions.
To get a umask value that results in -rw-r----- permissions, you subtract the desired permissions (640 in octal) from 666:

Calculate umask value
Full permissions (in octal) = 666
Desired permissions (in octal) = 640
umask value = Full permissions - Desired permissions = 666 - 640 = 026

Set the umask value
`$ umask 026`
This command sets the umask value to 026, which results in new files having -rw-r----- permissions.

Make this change permanent:

This change will only affect the current shell session. If you want to make this change permanent, you would need to add the umask 026 command to a shell startup file like ~/.bashrc or ~/.profile.

>mmmsub'

Question 27: Text Processing

In a Linux environment, you have a text file named letter that contains several occurrences of the string 'sam'. Your task is to replace each occurrence of 'sam' with 'Sam' and write the result to a new file named 'newletter'. Ensure that the original file letter remains unchanged.

Explanation

Use the sed command to replace 'sam' with 'Sam' and write the result to 'newletter'
```
$ sed 's/sam/Sam/g' letter > newletter
```

Explanation:

- The sed command is a stream editor for filtering and transforming text. The 's' in the sed command stands for substitute, 'sam' is the search string, 'Sam' is the replacement string, and 'g' stands for global, which means to replace all occurrences and not just the first one on each line.
- The > operator redirects the output to the file newletter. If newletter does not exist, it will be created; if it does exist, it will be overwritten. The original file letter remains unchanged.

Question 28: Shell Variable Scope

In a Linux environment, you have a shell variable named VARIABLE. Your task is to make this variable visible to subshells. This means that if you start a new shell from the current shell (a subshell), the VARIABLE should still be accessible.

Explanation

First, set the value of the variable. For example:
```
$ VARIABLE="value"
```

To make VARIABLE visible to subshells, you need to export it:
```
$ export VARIABLE
```
This commands first sets a value for VARIABLE, then exports it using the export command.

Explanation:

When a variable is exported, it is passed to child processes of the current shell. This means that if you start a new shell (a subshell), the VARIABLE will still be accessible. You can verify this by starting a new shell with the bash command, then using the echo command to print the value of VARIABLE.

Make this change permanent:

Please note that this change will only affect the current shell session and any subshells started from it. If you want to make this change permanent, you would need to add the export VARIABLE command to a shell startup file like ~/.bashrc or ~/.profile.

Question 29: System and Hardware Clock Synchronization

As a system administrator, you are required to synchronize the hardware clock with the system clock on a Linux server.

Explanation

The hardware clock, also known as the BIOS (Basic Input/Output System) clock or CMOS (Complementary Metal-Oxide-Semiconductor) clock, is independent of the operating system and continues to run even when the system is not powered on. The system clock, on the other hand, is controlled by the operating system and starts at each boot.

To synchronize the hardware clock with the system clock, you can use the hwclock command, which is a tool for accessing the hardware clock. You can run it in the terminal with sudo privileges:

```
$ sudo hwclock --systohc
```

This command sets the hardware clock to the current system time. The --systohc flag tells hwclock to set the hardware clock to the system time.

Question 30: Docker Container Management

You'll be working with Docker containers on your system. Your tasks are as follows:

1. Create and Run an Nginx Container:

- Create a new Docker container based on the nginx image. Assign a name my_nginx to the container for easier management.
- The container should run in the background and be configured to restart automatically on system reboots.

2. List and Prune Docker Images:

- List all Docker images currently available on the system.
- Remove all Docker images except for the nginx image.

3. Verify Changes:

- Verify that the nginx container is running and configured to restart on reboots.
- Verify the remaining Docker images on the system.

Explanation

1. Create and Run an Nginx Container:

First, pull the nginx image from Docker Hub (if not already available locally):
`$ docker pull nginx`

Next, create and run the Docker container based on the nginx

image:
```
$ docker run -d --name my_nginx --restart unless-stopped nginx
```

\# *-d:* Runs the container in detached mode (in the background).
\# *--name my_nginx:* Assigns a name to the container for easier management.
\# *--restart unless-stopped:* Configures the container to restart automatically on system reboots unless it is explicitly stopped.

Verification:
```
$ docker ps -a
```

Ensure the output shows the my_nginx container running with a status of Up and the restart policy set to unless-stopped.

2. List and Prune Docker Images:

List all Docker images on the system:
```
$ docker images
```

Remove all Docker images except for nginx. First, identify the image IDs of all images except for nginx:
```
$ docker images | grep -v 'nginx' | awk 'NR>1 {print $3}'
```
This command excludes the nginx image from the list and retrieves the image IDs of the remaining images.

Next, remove the identified images:
```
$ docker rmi $(docker images | grep -v 'nginx' | awk 'NR>1 {print $3}')
```

Verification:
```
$ docker images
```

Ensure the output shows only the nginx image remaining.

Question 31: Package and Service Management

You'll be working with the Nginx web server on your Linux system. Your tasks are as follows:

1. Install the Nginx Package:
Install the Nginx software package using the appropriate package manager for your system.

2. Enable Nginx at Boot:
Configure the system to automatically start the Nginx service during system boot.

3. Start the Nginx Service:
Start the Nginx service immediately to make it active.

4. Verify the Nginx Installation and Configuration:
Verify that Nginx is installed correctly, is set to start on boot, and is currently running.

Explanation

1. Install the Nginx Package:

The method to install Nginx depends on your Linux distribution. Below are the commands for common distributions:

For Debian-based systems (e.g., Ubuntu):
```
$ sudo apt update
$ sudo apt install nginx -y
```

For Red Hat-based systems (e.g., CentOS, Fedora, RHEL):

```
$ sudo yum install nginx -y
```

or for newer versions:
```
$ sudo dnf install nginx -y
```

2. Enable Nginx at Boot:

Enable the Nginx service to start automatically at boot time:
```
$ sudo systemctl enable nginx
```

3. Start the Nginx Service:

Start the Nginx service immediately:
```
$ sudo systemctl start nginx
```

4. Verify the Nginx Installation and Configuration:

Check if Nginx is installed:
```
$ nginx -v
```
This command should display the version of Nginx installed.

Verify Nginx service status:
```
$ sudo systemctl status nginx
```
This command should show that the Nginx service is active (running) and enabled (set to start at boot).

Ensure Nginx is set to start at boot:
```
$ sudo systemctl is-enabled nginx
```

The output should be:
```
enabled
```

Check if Nginx is running:
```
$ sudo systemctl is-active nginx
```

The output should be:

active

Question 32: File Compression and Extraction

Within your home directory, there are two compressed files: archive.tar.gz and archive.zip. Perform the following tasks:

1. Extract Contents of archive.tar.gz:
- Extract the contents of archive.tar.gz into a directory named /opt/restored_tar/.
- If the directory /opt/restored_tar/ does not exist, create it before extraction.

2. Extract Contents of archive.zip:
- Extract the contents of archive.zip into a directory named /opt/restored_zip/.
- If the directory /opt/restored_zip/ does not exist, create it before extraction.

3. Verify Extraction:
- Ensure the contents of both archives have been successfully extracted into their respective directories.

Explanation

1. Extract Contents of archive.tar.gz:

First, check if the directory /opt/restored_tar/ exists. If not, create it:
```
$ sudo mkdir -p /opt/restored_tar/
```

Next, extract the contents of archive.tar.gz into /opt/restored_tar/:
```
$ sudo tar -xzvf ~/archive.tar.gz -C /opt/restored_tar/
```

sudo: Ensures you have the necessary permissions to create directories and extract files into /opt/.
tar: The command used for working with tar files.
-x: Extracts the archive.
-z: Filters the archive through gzip.
-v: Verbosely lists files processed.
-f: Specifies the name of the archive file.
-C /opt/restored_tar/: Changes to the directory /opt/restored_tar/ before performing any operations.

2. Extract Contents of archive.zip:

Check if the directory /opt/restored_zip/ exists. If not, create it:
$ sudo mkdir -p /opt/restored_zip/

Then, extract the contents of archive.zip into /opt/restored_zip/:
$ sudo unzip ~/archive.zip -d /opt/restored_zip/

sudo: Ensures you have the necessary permissions to create directories and extract files into /opt/.
unzip: The command used for extracting .zip files.
-d /opt/restored_zip/: Specifies the target directory for the extraction.

3. Verify Extraction:

To ensure the contents have been successfully extracted, list the files in each target directory:

For /opt/restored_tar/:
$ ls /opt/restored_tar/

For /opt/restored_zip/:
$ ls /opt/restored_zip/

Question 33: File Permissions and Management

Assume there are 100 files in the /opt/database/ directory. Execute the following tasks:

1. Identify Executable Files:
- Identify all files in /opt/database/ where the owner has the executable permission enabled.
- Redirect the output (list of files) to /opt/executables.txt.

2. Remove SETUID Files:
- Discover all files with the SETUID permission enabled within the /opt/database/ directory, excluding subdirectories.
- Remove these files.

3. Duplicate Large Files:
- Find any file larger than 1MB within /opt/database/.
- Duplicate these files to /opt/.

Explanation

1. Identify Executable Files:

To find files where the owner has the executable permission enabled and redirect the output to /opt/executables.txt, use the following command:

```
$ find /opt/database/ -maxdepth 1 -type f -perm /u=x > /opt/executables.txt
```

find /opt/database/: The base command to search within the /opt/database/ directory.
-maxdepth 1: Limits the search to the specified directory, excluding subdirectories.

-*type f:* Restricts the search to files only.

-*perm /u=x:* Finds files where the owner has executable permissions.

> */opt/executables.txt:* Redirects the output to /opt/ executables.txt.

2. Remove SETUID Files:

To find and remove files with the SETUID permission enabled within /opt/database/ (excluding subdirectories), use:

$ find /opt/database/ -maxdepth 1 -type f -perm /4000 -exec rm -f {} \;

find /opt/database/: The base command to search within the / opt/database/ directory.

-*maxdepth 1:* Limits the search to the specified directory, excluding subdirectories.

-*type f:* Restricts the search to files only.

-*perm /4000:* Finds files with the SETUID bit set.

-*exec rm -f {} \;:* Executes the rm -f command on each found file to forcefully remove it.

3. Duplicate Large Files:

To find files larger than 1MB and duplicate them to /opt/, use:

$ find /opt/database/ -maxdepth 1 -type f -size +1M -exec cp {} /opt/ \;

find /opt/database/: The base command to search within the / opt/database/ directory.

-*maxdepth 1:* Limits the search to the specified directory, excluding subdirectories.

-*type f:* Restricts the search to files only.

-*size +1M:* Finds files larger than 1MB.

-*exec cp {} /opt/ \;:* Executes the cp command to copy each found file to the /opt/ directory.

Question 34: Automatically Mounting NFS Shares

As a system administrator, you've been assigned the following tasks:

1. Filesystem Configuration: Set up the system to automatically mount an NFS share at /mnt/nfsshare upon system boot.
2. NFS Share Creation: Establish an NFS share on a server with the IP address 192.168.1.100, exporting the directory /var/nfsshare.
3. NFS Client Configuration: Install necessary NFS packages on the client side.

Explanation

1. NFS Share Creation: First, on the NFS server (192.168.1.100), export the directory /var/nfsshare. Edit the /etc/exports file to include the following line:
/var/nfsshare 192.168.1.0/24(rw,sync,no_root_squash)
This line allows clients on the network 192.168.1.0/24 to mount /var/nfsshare with read-write access.

2. NFS Client Configuration: On the NFS client system, install the necessary NFS packages. Use the appropriate package manager for your distribution:

```
# For Debian/Ubuntu
$ sudo apt update
$ sudo apt install nfs-common

# For CentOS/RHEL
$ sudo yum install nfs-utils
```

These commands install the NFS client utilities required for mounting NFS shares.

3. Filesystem Configuration: To automatically mount the NFS share at /mnt/nfsshare upon system boot, you need to add an entry to the /etc/fstab file on the client system.

Open the /etc/fstab file in a text editor and add the following line:

```
192.168.1.100:/var/nfsshare /mnt/nfsshare nfs defaults 0 0
```

This line specifies that the NFS share located at 192.168.1.100:/var/nfsshare should be mounted at /mnt/nfsshare using the NFS filesystem type (nfs) with default mount options. The 0 0 at the end specifies options for dumping and filesystem checks, which are not necessary for NFS mounts.

Test Mounting: After adding the entry to /etc/fstab, you can test the mount without rebooting the system:

```
$ sudo mount -a
```

This command mounts all filesystems listed in /etc/fstab, including the NFS share specified for automatic mounting.

Verify Mount: To ensure that the NFS share is mounted successfully, you can check the mounted filesystems using the mount command:

```
$ mount | grep nfsshare
```

This command should display the NFS share mounted at /mnt/nfsshare.

Question 35: Essential Commands

As a system administrator, you're entrusted with executing fundamental Git operations to manage code repositories effectively. The tasks include:

1. Repository Initialization: Initialize a new Git repository.
2. New Branch Creation: Create a new branch `new-branch`, make changes, and merge branches.
3. Commit Changes: Commit the changes made on the new branch.
4. Push Changes: Push the changes to a remote repository.

Explanation

1. Repository Initialization:

To initiate a new Git repository, execute the git init command:
```
$ git init
```

2. New Branch Creation:

Create a new branch using git branch followed by the branch name, then switch to the new branch with git checkout:
```
$ git branch new-branch
$ git checkout new-branch
```

Making Changes:

Modify the files in the repository as necessary. After making changes, stage them for commit using git add. To stage all changes, utilize .:
```
$ git add .
```

3. Commit Changes:

Commit the changes on the new branch with git commit, specifying a commit message using the -m option:
$ git commit -m "Made some changes"

Merging Branches:

To merge the new branch into the main branch, switch back to the main branch using git checkout, then merge the new branch using git merge:
$ git checkout main
$ git merge new-branch

4. Push Changes:

Push the changes to a remote repository using git push. Specify the remote name (usually origin) and the branch name (usually main):
$ git push origin main

Question 36: Linux Command Line Interface (CLI) and I/O Redirection

Run a program named myapp and configure it such that its output is sent to both the standard output (stdout) and a file named myfile.log.

Explanation

1. Use the tee command to send output to both stdout and a file. The tee command reads from standard input and writes to standard output and files. In this case, you can use it to send the output of myapp to both stdout and myfile.log:
`$ myapp | tee myfile.log`

Explanation:

In this command, myapp is the program you're running, and | is a pipe that sends the output of myapp to tee. The tee command then writes the output to stdout and myfile.log.

2. To verify the operation, you can check the contents of myfile.log with the cat command:
`$ cat myfile.log`
This should display the same output that was printed to stdout when you ran myapp.

LFCS PRACTICE
EXAM SIX

Question 1: File Manipulation

1. Given a tar archive located at ~/data_archive.tar on your system, your objective is to extract its contents into a directory named ~/extracted_data. If ~/extracted_data doesn't exist, create it. Confirm the success of the extraction.

2. Adjust the permissions of the file ~/confidential.txt to grant read and write access for the owner and read-only access for the group. Confirm the success of the correct permissions modification.

Explanation

Task 1: Extract Contents of ~/data_archive.tar

1. Create the Extraction Directory (if it does not exist):

First, check if the directory ~/extracted_data exists. If not, create it:
```
$ mkdir -p ~/extracted_data
```

mkdir -p ~/extracted_data: Creates the directory ~/extracted_data if it doesn't exist. The -p option ensures no error is thrown if the directory already exists.

2. Extract the Tar Archive:

Extract the contents of ~/data_archive.tar into ~/extracted_data:
```
$ tar -xvf ~/data_archive.tar -C ~/extracted_data
```

tar: The command used for working with tar files.

-x: Extracts the archive.
-v: Verbosely lists files processed.
-f: Specifies the filename of the archive.
-C ~/extracted_data: Changes to the specified directory before performing any operations.

3. Confirm the Success of the Extraction:

List the contents of the extraction directory to ensure the files have been successfully extracted:
$ ls ~/extracted_data

Task 2: Adjust Permissions of ~/confidential.txt

1. Change File Permissions:

Adjust the permissions of the file ~/confidential.txt to grant read and write access for the owner and read-only access for the group:
$ chmod 640 ~/confidential.txt

chmod: Command to change file permissions.
640: Sets the permissions to rw-r----- (read and write for the owner, read-only for the group, and no permissions for others).

2. Confirm the Success of the Permissions Modification:

Verify the permissions of the file ~/confidential.txt:
$ ls -l ~/confidential.txt

ls -l ~/confidential.txt: Displays detailed information about the file, including its permissions. The output should show -rw-r----- indicating the correct permissions have been set.

Question 2: Package Management

As a system administrator, your task is to install the htop package on the system. Confirm the successful installation by verifying the installation process and ensuring that the htop command runs correctly.

Explanation

1. Update Package Lists:

Before installing any package, it's a good practice to update the package lists to ensure you have the latest information about available packages.

For Debian-based systems (e.g., Ubuntu):
$ sudo apt update

For Red Hat-based systems (e.g., CentOS, Fedora, RHEL):
$ sudo yum check-update

2. Install htop Package:

Install the htop package using the appropriate package manager for your system.

For Debian-based systems (e.g., Ubuntu):
$ sudo apt install htop -y

sudo: Runs the command with superuser privileges.
apt install htop: Installs the htop package.
-y: Automatically answers 'yes' to prompts during the installation.

For Red Hat-based systems (e.g., CentOS, Fedora, RHEL):
`$ sudo yum install htop -y`

or for newer versions:
`$ sudo dnf install htop -y`

3. Confirm the Installation:

Verify the installation by checking the package information and ensuring that htop runs correctly.

Check if htop is installed:
`$ htop --version`
This command should display the version of htop installed, indicating that the package is correctly installed.

Run htop:
`$ htop`
This command should launch the htop interactive process viewer. If htop starts without errors, it confirms that the installation is successful.

Question 3: Cron Job Management

Task:

1. Create a Backup Script:

Write a shell script named ~/weekly_backup.sh that performs the following actions:

- Backs up the ~/important_files directory.
- Creates a compressed archive (tar.gz) with a timestamp in the filename.
- Saves the archive in the ~/backup directory. If the ~/backup directory does not exist, create it.

2. Schedule a Cron Job:

- Configure a cron job to run the ~/weekly_backup.sh script every Sunday at 2:00 AM.

Explanation

Step 1: Create the Backup Script

1. Create the ~/backup Directory (if it does not exist):

Ensure the backup directory exists in the script. If it doesn't, create it:
$ mkdir -p ~/backup

2. Create the Shell Script:

Write the ~/weekly_backup.sh script with the necessary commands to back up the ~/important_files directory and create a timestamped compressed archive.

```
#!/bin/bash

# Define source and destination directories
SOURCE_DIR=~/important_files
BACKUP_DIR=~/backup

# Ensure the backup directory exists
mkdir -p $BACKUP_DIR

# Create a timestamped filename for the backup
TIMESTAMP=$(date +'%Y%m%d_%H%M%S')
BACKUP_FILE=$BACKUP_DIR/important_files_backup_
$TIMESTAMP.tar.gz

# Create the compressed archive
tar -czf $BACKUP_FILE -C $SOURCE_DIR .

# Confirm completion
echo "Backup completed successfully: $BACKUP_FILE"
```

Save this script as ~/weekly_backup.sh.

2. Make the Script Executable:

Change the script permissions to make it executable:
```
$ chmod +x ~/weekly_backup.sh
```

Step 2: Schedule the Cron Job

1. Edit the Cron Table:

Open the cron table for editing:
```
$ crontab -e
```

2. Add the Cron Job:

Add the following line to schedule the script to run every Sunday at 2:00 AM:
`0 2 * * 0 ~/weekly_backup.sh`

*0 2 * * 0:* Specifies the schedule (minute, hour, day of month, month, day of week). This means:
0: At minute 0.
2: At 2 AM.
**:* Every day of the month.
**:* Every month.
0: On Sunday (0 represents Sunday in the cron syntax).

3. Save and Exit:

Save the changes and exit the editor. The cron job is now scheduled.

Question 4: User and Group Management

Task:

1. Create a New Group:
Create a new group named finance.

2. Create a New User (if necessary):
Check if the user accountant exists. If not, create this user.

3. Add the User to the Group:
Add the user accountant to the finance group.

Explanation

Step 1: Create a New Group

Create the finance Group:

Use the groupadd command to create a new group named finance:
`$ sudo groupadd finance`

Step 2: Create a New User (if necessary)

1. Check if the User accountant Exists:

Use the id command to check if the user accountant exists:
`$ id accountant`

- If the user exists, the command will return information about the user.
- If the user does not exist, the command will return an error.

2. Create the User accountant (if necessary):

If the user accountant does not exist, create the user using the useradd command:
```
$ sudo useradd accountant
```

Optionally, set a password for the new user:
```
$ sudo passwd accountant
```

Step 3: Add the User to the Group

Add the User accountant to the finance Group:

Use the usermod command to add the user accountant to the finance group:
```
$ sudo usermod -aG finance accountant
```

-aG: Appends the user to the supplementary group without removing the user from other groups.

Question 5: Automation and Configuration Management

Task:

Create a Bash script named ~/monitor_system.sh that gathers system information, including CPU usage, memory usage, and disk space. This script should append this data to a file named ~/sys-info. Ensure that the script can be executed multiple times, with each run appending new information to the file without removing the old data. If the file ~/sys-info does not exist, the script should create it.

Explanation

Step 1: Create the Bash Script

1. Create the ~/monitor_system.sh Script:

Create a new file named monitor_system.sh in the home directory (~/) and open it in a text editor:
```
$ vim ~/monitor_system.sh
```

2. Write the Script:

Write the script to gather system information and append it to the ~/sys-info file:

```
#!/bin/bash

# File path for storing system information
SYS_INFO=~/sys-info

# Check if the sys-info file exists, create if not
```

```
if [ ! -f "$SYS_INFO" ]; then
  touch $SYS_INFO
fi

# Gather system information and append to the sys-info file
{
  echo "========== $(date) =========="
  echo "CPU Usage:"
  top -b -n1 | grep "Cpu(s)"
  echo ""
  echo "Memory Usage:"
  free -h
  echo ""
  echo "Disk Space:"
  df -h
  echo "============================="
} >> $SYS_INFO
```

3. Make the Script Executable:

Change the script permissions to make it executable:

```
$ chmod +x ~/monitor_system.sh
```

Question 6: System Configuration

Task:

Customize the system's login message to display the announcement "Please be advised that there will be a scheduled system maintenance on Sunday, May 5, 2024, from 2:00 AM to 4:00 AM." Ensure visibility to all users upon login, irrespective of the login method used (Console, SSH).

Explanation

Step 1: Edit the Login Message Configuration

1. Open the motd File:

The motd file in the /etc/ directory contains the Message of the Day that is displayed to users upon login. Open it for editing:
$ sudo nano /etc/motd

2. Write the Login Message:

Add the desired login message to the file. In this case, add the maintenance announcement:
"Please be advised that there will be a scheduled system maintenance on Sunday, May 5, 2024, from 2:00 AM to 4:00 AM."

Press Ctrl + X to exit, then press Y to save the changes.

Question 7: Process Management

Task:

Send a SIGHUP signal to the process named "java_app".

Explanation

Step 1: Identify the Process ID (PID) of "java_app"

Use the pgrep Command to Find the PID:

Use the pgrep command to find the PID of the process named "java_app":
```
$ pgrep java_app
```
This command will return the PID of the "java_app" process.

Step 2: Send the SIGHUP Signal

Use the kill Command to Send the SIGHUP Signal:

Once you have the PID of the "java_app" process, use the kill command to send the SIGHUP signal:
```
$ kill -HUP PID
```
Replace PID with the actual PID of the "java_app" process obtained in Step 1.

Question 8: Storage Management

Task:

Your task is to create a new partition on the /dev/sdf disk. The partition should be named /dev/sdf1, have a size of 1GB, and be formatted with the XFS filesystem. Ensure that there is sufficient unallocated space on the /dev/sdf disk before creating the new partition. If the partition /dev/sdf1 already exists, delete it before creating the new one.

Explanation

Step 1: Check Disk Space and Existing Partitions

1. Use the lsblk Command to Check Disk Space:

Check the disk space on /dev/sdf to ensure there is sufficient unallocated space:
`$ lsblk /dev/sdf`
Ensure there is enough unallocated space to create a 1GB partition.

2. Use the ls Command to Check Existing Partitions:

Check if the /dev/sdf1 partition already exists:
`$ ls /dev/sdf1`
If the partition exists, proceed to Step 2 to delete it.

Step 2: Delete Existing Partition (If Necessary)

1. Use the fdisk Command to Delete the Partition:

Delete the existing /dev/sdf1 partition using the fdisk

command:
`$ sudo fdisk /dev/sdf`

- Press d to delete a partition.
- Choose the appropriate partition number (usually 1 for /dev/sdf1).
- Press w to save the changes and exit.

Step 3: Create New Partition and Format

1. Use the fdisk Command to Create a New Partition:

Create a new 1GB partition named /dev/sdf1 using the fdisk command:
`$ sudo fdisk /dev/sdf`

- Press n to create a new partition.
- Choose the partition type (usually primary).
- Specify the partition size (1GB).
- Press w to save the changes and exit.

2. Format the Partition with the XFS Filesystem:

Format the newly created partition /dev/sdf1 with the XFS filesystem:
`$ sudo mkfs.xfs /dev/sdf1`

Question 9: Archives and Compression

Task:

Your task is to create a compressed tar archive of the entire /etc directory. The compressed archive should be named etc_backup.tar.xz and moved to a directory named /backup_etc. Ensure the /backup_etc directory exists, and if not, create it. Ensure that the compression is performed using the xz compression algorithm.

Explanation

Step 1: Create the Backup Directory

Create the /backup_etc directory:
```
$ sudo mkdir /backup_etc
```
This command creates the /backup_etc directory if it doesn't already exist.

Step 2: Create the Compressed Tar Archive

Use the tar Command to Create the Archive:

Create a compressed tar archive of the /etc directory named etc_backup.tar.xz:
```
$ sudo tar -cJf /backup_etc/etc_backup.tar.xz /etc
```

-c: Create a new archive.
-J: Use the xz compression algorithm.
-f: Specifies the filename of the archive.

Question 10: File Operations

Task:

You need to identify and list all files in the current user's home directory that are greater than 5 MB in size. Subsequently, move these files to a new directory named m5mb-files within the user's home directory. If the m5mb-files directory does not exist, create it.

Explanation

Step 1: Identify Files Greater Than 5MB

Use the find Command to Identify Files:

Identify all files in the current user's home directory ($HOME) that are greater than 5MB in size:
```
$ find $HOME -type f -size +5M
```
This command lists all files (-type f) in the user's home directory that are greater than 5MB in size (-size +5M).

Step 2: Create the Destination Directory

Check if m5mb-files Directory Exists:

Check if the m5mb-files directory already exists:

```
if [ ! -d "$HOME/m5mb-files" ]; then
    mkdir $HOME/m5mb-files
fi
```
This command creates the m5mb-files directory within the user's home directory if it doesn't already exist.

Step 3: Move Identified Files

Use the mv Command to Move Files:

Move the identified files to the m5mb-files directory:
$ find $HOME -type f -size +5M -exec mv -t $HOME/m5mb-files {} +

 # find $HOME -type f -size +5M: Finds all files greater than 5MB in size within the user's home directory.
 # -exec mv -t $HOME/m5mb-files {} +: Executes the mv command to move the identified files to the m5mb-files directory.

Question 11: Setting Default Kernel

Task:

Set kernel number 1 (referring to its position in the GRUB menu, not the actual kernel version number) as the default boot option.

Explanation

Step 1: Identify the GRUB Configuration File

Locate the GRUB Configuration File:

Locate the GRUB configuration file, typically located at /etc/default/grub:
```
$ sudo nano /etc/default/grub
```

Step 2: Set the Default Kernel

Edit the GRUB Configuration File:

Modify the GRUB_DEFAULT parameter to set the default boot option to kernel number 1:
```
GRUB_DEFAULT=1
```

Step 3: Update GRUB Configuration

Update GRUB Configuration:

After saving the changes, update the GRUB configuration to apply the changes:
```
$ sudo update-grub
```

Question 12: Networking Configuration

Task:

Configure a static IP address of 192.168.2.100 with a subnet mask of 255.255.255.0 and a default gateway of 192.168.2.1 for the network interface named ens3. Additionally, set preferred and alternate DNS servers for proper internet resolution.

Explanation

Step 1: Configure Static IP Address, Subnet Mask, and Default Gateway

1. Edit the Network Configuration File:

Open the network configuration file for editing, typically located at /etc/network/interfaces or /etc/sysconfig/network-scripts/ifcfg-ens3 depending on the Linux distribution:
$ sudo nano /etc/network/interfaces
or
$ sudo nano /etc/sysconfig/network-scripts/ifcfg-ens3

2. Configure Static IP Address, Subnet Mask, and Default Gateway:

Add or modify the configuration parameters to set the static IP address, subnet mask, and default gateway:

```
iface ens3 inet static
   address 192.168.2.100
   netmask 255.255.255.0
```

    gateway 192.168.2.1

Step 2: Configure DNS Servers

1. Edit the DNS Configuration File:

Open the DNS configuration file for editing, typically located at /etc/resolv.conf:
```
$ sudo nano /etc/resolv.conf
```

2. Set Preferred and Alternate DNS Servers:

Add the IP addresses of the preferred and alternate DNS servers:
```
nameserver 8.8.8.8
nameserver 8.8.4.4
```

Step 3: Apply the Network Configuration Changes

1. Restart the Network Service:

Restart the network service to apply the changes:
```
$ sudo systemctl restart networking
```
or
```
$ sudo systemctl restart network
```

Question 13: Storage Management

Task:

Reduce the size of the logical volume named "data_vol" within the volume group "vg03" by 200MB. Assuming the filesystem on the logical volume is already unmounted.

Explanation

Step 1: Check Logical Volume Size

Use the lvdisplay Command to Check Logical Volume Size:

Check the current size of the logical volume "data_vol" within the volume group "vg03":
```
$ sudo lvdisplay /dev/vg03/data_vol
```

Step 2: Reduce Logical Volume Size

Use the lvreduce Command to Reduce Logical Volume Size:

Reduce the size of the logical volume "data_vol" within the volume group "vg03" by 200MB:
```
$ sudo lvreduce -L -200M /dev/vg03/data_vol
```

Question 14: Advanced Networking Configuration

Task:

Create a firewall rule to allow incoming traffic on TCP port 8080. Ensure the rule persists after the system reboots.

Explanation

Step 1: Add Firewall Rule

Use the iptables Command to Add Firewall Rule:

Add a firewall rule to allow incoming traffic on TCP port 8080:
```
$ sudo iptables -A INPUT -p tcp --dport 8080 -j ACCEPT
```

Step 2: Save Firewall Rules

Use the iptables-save Command to Save Rules:

Save the current firewall rules to a file:
```
$ sudo iptables-save > /etc/iptables/rules.v4
```

Question 15: Container Configuration and Management

Task:

1. Install Docker Engine on the system.
2. Pull the official Ubuntu image from Docker Hub.
3. Run a container based on the Ubuntu image named "ubuntu_server".

Explanation

Step 1: Install Docker Engine

1. Install Docker Engine:

Install Docker Engine using the appropriate package manager for your system. For example, on Debian-based systems:
$ sudo apt-get update
$ sudo apt-get install docker.io

Step 2: Pull Ubuntu Image

Pull Official Ubuntu Image:

Pull the official Ubuntu image from Docker Hub:
$ sudo docker pull ubuntu

Step 3: Run Container

Run Container Based on Ubuntu Image:

Run a container based on the Ubuntu image named "ubuntu_server":

```
$ sudo docker run --name ubuntu_server -d ubuntu
```

Question 16: Database
Management

Task:

1. Connect to the MySQL server as a privileged user.
2. Create a new database named "salesdb".
3. Create a user named "salesuser" and grant them access to the "salesdb" database with a password of "salespass".

Explanation

Step 1: Connect to MySQL Server

Connect to MySQL Server:

Connect to the MySQL server as a privileged user. Depending on your MySQL setup, you may need to use the mysql command with appropriate credentials:
```
$ mysql -u root -p
```
Enter the password when prompted.

Step 2: Create Database

Create Database:

Inside the MySQL shell, create a new database named "salesdb":
```
CREATE DATABASE salesdb;
```

Step 3: Create User and Grant Privileges

Create User and Grant Privileges:

Still within the MySQL shell, create a new user named

"salesuser" with the password "salespass" and grant them access to the "salesdb" database:

```
CREATE USER 'salesuser'@'localhost' IDENTIFIED BY 'salespass';
GRANT ALL PRIVILEGES ON salesdb.* TO 'salesuser'@'localhost';
```

Question 17: Network Configuration and Management

Task:

1. SSH to Node1 as user "Sam" with password "system".
2. Add an additional DNS server (nameserver) of 8.8.8.8.
3. Add a static host entry for "dbserver" resolving to 192.168.69.12.
4. Find the IP address of the eth2 interface and add a temporary static route for the network 192.168.69.3/24 via the eth2 interface IP address.

Explanation

Step 1: SSH to Node1 as User "Sam"

SSH to Node1 as User "Sam":

Connect to Node1 via SSH as user "Sam" with the password "system":
```
$ ssh Sam@Node1
```

Step 2: Add Additional DNS Server

Edit DNS Configuration File:

Open the DNS configuration file for editing:
```
$ sudo vim /etc/resolv.conf
```

Add Additional DNS Server:

Append the IP address of the additional DNS server (8.8.8.8) to the file:

nameserver 8.8.8.8

Step 3: Add Static Host Entry

Edit Hosts File:

Open the hosts file for editing:
$ sudo vim /etc/hosts

Add Static Host Entry:

Append a static host entry for "dbserver" resolving to
192.168.69.12:
192.168.69.12 dbserver

Step 4: Add Temporary Static Route

Find IP Address of eth2 Interface:

Use the ip addr command to find the IP address of the eth2
interface:
$ ip addr show eth2

Add Temporary Static Route:

Add a temporary static route for the network 192.168.69.3/24
via the eth2 interface IP address (assuming the eth2 IP is
192.168.69.1):
$ sudo ip route add 192.168.69.3/24 via 192.168.69.1

Question 18: File Manipulation

Task:

Assume you have a file located at /opt/test. Your task is to create a hard link to this file in the /home/Sam directory with the name test. Ensure that the hard link remains functional even after the system reboots.

Explanation

1. A hard link is essentially a directory entry, or pointer, to the data on the disk. It's not a copy of the file, but a pointer to the original data:

Here's how you can create a hard link:
```
$ ln /opt/test /home/Sam/test
```
This command creates a hard link at /home/Sam/test that points to the same data as /opt/test.

2. To verify that the hard link was created successfully, you can use the ls -l command:
```
$ ls -l /home/Sam/test
```
The number in the second field of the output represents the number of hard links that exist for the file. If the hard link was created successfully, this number should be 2 (one for the original file and one for the hard link).

Question 19: File Manipulation

Task:

Assume you have a file located at /home/Sam/sample. Your task is to create a soft link (symbolic link) at /var/sample that points to this file. Ensure that the soft link remains functional even after the system reboots.

Explanation

A soft link, also known as a symbolic link, is a special kind of file that points to another file or directory. It's a way to create a shortcut to the original file or directory.

1. Here's how you can create a soft link:
```
$ ln -s /home/Sam/sample /var/sample
```
This command creates a soft link at /var/sample that points to the file at /home/Sam/sample.

2. To verify that the soft link was created successfully, you can use the ls -l command:
```
$ ls -l /var/sample
```
The output should show /var/sample -> /home/Sam/sample, indicating that /var/sample is a soft link to /home/Sam/sample.

This change is permanent and will persist across system reboots because soft links are stored on the disk, and the filesystem maintains the link even after the system is rebooted.

Question 20: File Ownership and Permissions

Tasks: In your home directory, there is a file named important_data.txt. Execute the following actions on this file:

1. Change the ownership of this file to the user Sam and the group devops.
2. Modify the permissions of this file such that:
3. User Sam has read, write, and execute permissions.
4. Group devops has read and write permissions, but not execute permission.
5. All other users have only read permission.
6. Enable the SUID (set user id) special permission on important_data.txt. This means that when the file is executed, it will run with the user ID of the owner of the file, rather than the user ID of the person running it.

Explanation

1. To change the ownership of the file to user Sam and group devops, utilize the chown command:
$ sudo chown Sam:devops ~/important_data.txt

Explanation: This command alters the user and group ownership of a given file. Sam:devops specifies the new user and group, and ~/important_data.txt is the file path.

2. To adjust the permissions of the file, use the chmod command:
$ sudo chmod 751 ~/important_data.txt

Explanation: This command sets the permissions of the file. 751 specifies read, write, and execute permissions for the user

(7), read and write permissions for the group (5), and read permission for others (1).

3. To enable the SUID special permission on the file, employ the chmod command again:

```
$ sudo chmod u+s ~/important_data.txt
```

Explanation: This command sets the SUID bit on the file, ensuring that when it is executed, it runs with the user ID of the owner of the file.

Verify the ownership and permissions of the file using ls -l ~/important_data.txt to confirm success:

```
$ ls -l ~/important_data.txt
```

This command will display the ownership and permissions of the file. If successful, you should see the new ownership and permissions.

Question 21: File and Directory Operations

Tasks: In your home directory, there are three files named report1.txt, report2.txt, and report3.txt. Perform the following actions:

1. Create a new directory at /opt/reports/.
2. Move the file report1.txt from your home directory to the /opt/reports/ directory.
3. Copy the file report2.txt from your home directory to the /opt/reports/ directory.
4. Delete the file report3.txt from your home directory.

Explanation

1. To create the directory /opt/reports/, employ the mkdir command:
`$ sudo mkdir /opt/reports/`

Explanation: This command creates a new directory. /opt/reports/ specifies the path of the new directory.

2. To move report1.txt to the /opt/reports/ directory, utilize the mv command:
`$ mv ~/report1.txt /opt/reports/`

Explanation: The mv command moves a file from one location to another. ~/report1.txt specifies the path of the file to be moved, and /opt/reports/ specifies the destination directory.

3. To copy report2.txt to the /opt/reports/ directory, use the cp command:
`$ cp ~/report2.txt /opt/reports/`

Explanation: The cp command copies a file from one location to another. ~/report2.txt specifies the path of the file to be copied, and /opt/reports/ specifies the destination directory.

4. To remove report3.txt, employ the rm command:
$ rm ~/report3.txt

Explanation: The rm command removes a file. ~/report3.txt specifies the path of the file to be removed.

Verify the contents of the /opt/reports/ directory using ls /opt/reports/ to confirm success:
$ ls /opt/reports/
This command will display the contents of the /opt/reports/ directory. If successful, you should see report1.txt and report2.txt in the directory.

Question 22: Archive Creation and Compression

In this exercise, you'll perform various archiving and compression tasks for the /opt/backup/ directory:

1. Create a simple TAR archive (uncompressed) that contains all files in the /opt/backup/ directory. Store this archive at /opt/backup.tar.
2. Compress the entire /opt/backup/ directory into a GZipped TAR archive. Store this archive at /opt/backup.tar.gz.
3. Compress the entire /opt/backup/ directory into a BZipped TAR archive. Store this archive at /opt/backup.tar.bz2.
4. Create a non-TAR archive. This time, create a simple compressed ZIP archive of /opt/backup/ and store this archive at /opt/backup.zip.

Explanation

1. To create a simple TAR archive containing all files in the /opt/backup/ directory, use the tar command:
$ tar -cf /opt/backup.tar /opt/backup/

Explanation:

tar is the command-line utility for archiving files.
-cf flags are used to create a new archive file.
/opt/backup.tar specifies the name and location of the output archive.
/opt/backup/ specifies the directory to be archived.

2. To compress the entire /opt/backup/ directory into a GZipped TAR archive, use:
$ tar -czf /opt/backup.tar.gz /opt/backup/

Explanation:

-czf flags are used to create a new GZipped TAR archive. */opt/backup.tar.gz* specifies the name and location of the output archive.

3. To compress the entire /opt/backup/ directory into a BZipped TAR archive, use:

`$ tar -cjf /opt/backup.tar.bz2 /opt/backup/`

Explanation:

-cjf flags are used to create a new BZipped TAR archive. */opt/backup.tar.bz2* specifies the name and location of the output archive.

4. To create a non-TAR archive, specifically a ZIP archive of /opt/backup/, use:
`$ zip -r /opt/backup.zip /opt/backup/`

Explanation:

zip is the command-line utility for creating ZIP archives.
-r flag recursively includes all files and directories under /opt/backup/.
/opt/backup.zip specifies the name and location of the output ZIP archive.

Verify the creation of archives using ls:
`$ ls -l /opt/`
This command will list all files in the /opt/ directory, including the newly created archives. If successful, you should see backup.tar, backup.tar.gz, backup.tar.bz2, and backup.zip among the listed files.

Question 23: Shell Scripting
and User Management

Task: On a system named ServerA, write a shell script named "~/users_shells.sh". This script should generate a list of usernames from the passwd file in the /etc/ directory along with their corresponding login shells.

Explanation

1. To create the script file "~/users_shells.sh", run:
`$ vim /users_shells.sh`

2. Switch the file to the editing mode by pressing the I key, then type the following bold lines:

To specify the interpreter that should be used to execute the script, type:

`#!/bin/bash`

To generate a list of usernames from the passwd file in the / etc/ directory along with their login shell, type:

`cut -d: -f1,7 /etc/passwd`

3. Press Esc to switch to command mode, then type :wq followed by Enter to save and exit.

4. To run the shell script "/users_shells.sh", use:
`$ sh /users_shells.sh`

Question 24: System Administration - Master Boot Record Backup

Task: Using appropriate commands, create a backup of the Master Boot Record (MBR) located on the device "/dev/sda" of ServerA. Store the backup in the file "/backup/mbr.img". Ensure the backup process adheres to the following requirements:

Block Size: 512 bytes
Number of Blocks Copied: 1
Verification: Confirm successful backup creation

Explanation

1. Create the Backup Directory:
$ sudo mkdir -p /backup
The -p flag ensures the directory is created, even if it already exists, preventing errors.

2. Perform MBR Backup:
$ sudo dd if=/dev/sda of=/backup/mbr.img bs=512 count=1 status=progress

if=/dev/sda: Specifies the input file, which is the entire first hard disk.
of=/backup/mbr.img: Specifies the output file, where the MBR backup will be stored.
bs=512: Sets the block size to 512 bytes, matching the MBR size.
count=1: Copies only 1 block, ensuring only the MBR is backed up.
status=progress: Displays progress during the backup process,

providing visibility.

3. Verify Backup Creation:
`$ ls -l /backup/mbr.img`

ls -l: Lists detailed information about the backup file, including its size and permissions.

Question 25: System Boot Configuration - Multi-User Target

Task: Configure ServerA, to automatically boot into the multi-user.target, ensuring a non-graphical, multi-user environment for command-line administration.

Explanation

1. Check Current Default Target:
$ systemctl get-default

2. Set Multi-User Target as Default:
$ sudo systemctl set-default multi-user.target

3. Verify Default Target:
$ systemctl get-default

Question 26: System Configuration Challenge

Configure a custom prompt for the Bash shell that displays the current username and hostname. Ensure that the custom prompt remains persistent across reboots.

Explanation

Step 1: Open the Bash configuration file

Use a text editor like vim to open the Bash configuration file.
`$ vim ~/.bashrc`

Step 2: Add the custom prompt configuration

Append the following line at the end of the file to set up a custom prompt showing the username and hostname.
`echo 'export PS1="\u@\h:\w\$ "' >> ~/.bashrc`

Step 3: Apply the changes

Source the Bash configuration file to apply the changes immediately.
`$ source ~/.bashrc`

Explanation:

- In Step 1, the Bash configuration file (~/.bashrc) is opened using a text editor. This file is read and executed by Bash every time a new session starts.
- In Step 2, a line is added to the end of the ~/.bashrc file to export a new value for the PS1 environment variable. This value defines the primary prompt string in Bash. The

\u, \h, and \w are special escape sequences representing the username, hostname, and current working directory, respectively.

- Finally, in Step 3, the source command is used to read and execute the content of the updated ~/.bashrc file. This ensures that the changes take effect immediately without the need to start a new session.

- These modifications persist across reboots because the ~/.bashrc file is read every time a new Bash session starts, ensuring that the custom prompt configuration remains consistent.

Question 27: Storage Management

Assuming you have root privileges, perform the following tasks using /dev/sdc:

1. Create a 4GiB LVM volume group named "vgroup".
2. Inside the "vgroup" LVM volume group, create a 1GiB LVM logical volume named "lvol".
3. Format the "lvol" LVM logical volume with the ext4 filesystem.
4. Mount the "lvol" LVM logical volume persistently on the "/lvol" directory. Ensure that the mount persists across reboots.
5. Extend the ext4 filesystem on "lvol" by 100M.

Note: If the "/lvol" directory does not exist, create it.

Explanation

1. Create a 4GiB LVM volume group named "vgroup"
pvcreate /dev/sdc
$ sudo vgcreate vgroup /dev/sdc

2. Within the "vgroup" LVM volume group, create a 1GiB LVM logical volume named "lvol"
$ sudo lvcreate -L 1G -n lvol vgroup

3. Format the "lvol" LVM logical volume with the ext4 filesystem
$ sudo mkfs.ext4 /dev/vgroup/lvol

4. Mount the "lvol" LVM logical volume persistently on the "/lvol" directory
$ sudo mkdir -p /lvol
$ sudo echo '/dev/vgroup/lvol /lvol ext4 defaults 0 0' >> /etc/

fstab
$ sudo mount -a

5. Extend the ext4 filesystem on "lvol" by 100M
$ sudo lvextend -L +100M /dev/vgroup/lvol
$ sudo resize2fs /dev/vgroup/lvol

Explanation:

- pvcreate: Initializes /dev/sdc for use by LVM.
- vgcreate: Creates a new volume group named "vgroup" using /dev/sdc.
- lvcreate: Creates a new logical volume named "lvol" within the "vgroup" volume group.
- mkfs.ext4: Formats the logical volume with the ext4 filesystem.
- mkdir -p /lvol: Creates the mount point directory if it doesn't exist.
- The echo command adds an entry to /etc/fstab to ensure the volume is mounted automatically at boot.
- mount -a: Mounts all filesystems mentioned in fstab.
- lvextend: Extends the size of the logical volume by 100M.
- resize2fs: Resizes the ext4 filesystem to utilize the additional space.

Question 28: Configure Automounter for an External USB Drive

Task:

Configure an automounter for an external USB drive to automatically mount at /mnt/usb when connected to the system. The filesystem on the USB drive is ext4, and the device name is /dev/sdb1. Ensure the mount persists across reboots and unmounts automatically when the drive is disconnected.

Explanation

Step 1: Install Automounter (if not installed)

1. Install Automounter:

If the automounter (usually autofs) is not installed on your system, install it using the appropriate package manager:

# For Debian/Ubuntu based systems
$ sudo apt-get install autofs

# For CentOS/RHEL based systems
$ sudo yum install autofs

Step 2: Configure Automounter

Edit Automounter Configuration File:

Open the automounter configuration file for editing (this may vary depending on the distribution):
$ sudo nano /etc/auto.master

Add Entry for USB Drive:

Append a line to the auto.master file to specify the mount point and configuration file for the USB drive:
/mnt/usb /etc/auto.usb --timeout=5

Create Automounter Configuration File:

Create a configuration file for the USB drive (/etc/auto.usb) and specify the mount options:
$ sudo nano /etc/auto.usb

Add the following line to the auto.usb file:
usb -fstype=ext4,rw :/dev/sdb1

Step 3: Restart Automounter Service

Restart Automounter Service:

Restart the automounter service to apply the changes:
$ sudo systemctl restart autofs   # For systemd-based systems

Question 29: Locate and List Recently Modified Files in /home Directory

Task:

Utilize the command line to locate and list all files in the /home directory that were modified within the last 3 days. Additionally, provide the total count of such files.

Explanation

Step 1: Locate Recently Modified Files

Use find Command:

Utilize the find command to search for files in the /home directory modified within the last 3 days:
`$ find /home -type f -mtime -3`

Step 2: List Recently Modified Files

List Files with Detailed Information:

Pipe the output of the find command to ls -l to list the recently modified files with detailed information:
`$ find /home -type f -mtime -3 -exec ls -l {} +`

Step 3: Count Recently Modified Files

Count Files:

Pipe the output of the find command to wc -l to count the number of recently modified files:

```
$ find /home -type f -mtime -3 | wc -l
```

Question 30: Setting Up a Firewall Rule for Incoming SSH Traffic

Task:

Utilize the command line to establish a basic firewall rule permitting incoming SSH traffic on port 22. Ensure the rule persists after the system reboots. Additionally, provide commands to confirm the rule's correctness and persistence after reboots. If any packages or services are necessary for this setup, please install them.

Explanation

Step 1: Install Firewall Management Tool (if not installed)

Install Firewall Management Tool:
If a firewall management tool (e.g., iptables, firewalld, ufw) is not installed on your system, install it using the appropriate package manager:

# For Debian/Ubuntu based systems
$ sudo apt-get install ufw

# For CentOS/RHEL based systems
$ sudo yum install firewalld

Step 2: Configure Firewall Rule

Allow SSH Traffic:
Add a rule to allow incoming SSH traffic on port 22:

# For iptables
$ sudo iptables -A INPUT -p tcp --dport 22 -j ACCEPT

For firewalld
```
$ sudo firewall-cmd --zone=public --add-port=22/tcp --permanent
```

For ufw
```
$ sudo ufw allow 22/tcp
```

Step 3: Ensure Persistence

Persist Firewall Rule:
Ensure that the firewall rule persists after system reboots:

For iptables
```
$ sudo iptables-save > /etc/iptables/rules.v4
```

For firewalld
```
$ sudo firewall-cmd --runtime-to-permanent
```

For ufw
```
$ sudo ufw enable
```

Step 4: Confirm Rule's Correctness and Persistence

Confirm Rule's Correctness:
Verify that the firewall rule allowing SSH traffic on port 22 is correctly configured:

For iptables
```
$ sudo iptables -L INPUT
```

For firewalld
```
$ sudo firewall-cmd --list-all
```

For ufw
```
$ sudo ufw status
```

Confirm Rule's Persistence:

Ensure that the firewall rule persists after system reboots:

```
# For iptables
$ cat /etc/iptables/rules.v4
```

```
# For firewalld
$ sudo firewall-cmd --permanent --list-all
```

```
# For ufw
$ sudo ufw status
```

Question 31: File System Permissions and Group Ownership

On a Linux server, your task is to create a directory named "/collaboration". Configure the permissions of this directory such that any files or subdirectories created within it are owned by the group "managers".

Explanation

1. Create the "/collaboration" directory:
$ sudo mkdir /collaboration

2. Change the group ownership of the directory to "managers":
$ sudo chgrp managers /collaboration

3. Set the setgid bit on the directory. This will cause any files or subdirectories created within "/collaboration" to inherit the group ownership:
$ sudo chmod g+s /collaboration

4. To verify that the directory has been correctly configured, you can use the ls command with the -ld option, which displays information about directories:
$ ls -ld /collaboration
This command should show that the group owner of "/collaboration" is "managers" and that the setgid bit is set (indicated by an "s" in the group permissions).

Question 32: File System Links

On a Linux server, your task is to create a hard link and a symbolic link to a file named "data.txt". The original file is located in the /home/$USER/ directory. The hard link should be created in the same directory as the original file, while the symbolic link should be created in the /var/tmp/ directory.

Explanation

1. Create a hard link to "data.txt" in the same directory:
$ ln /home/$USER/data.txt /home/$USER/data_hardlink.txt

2. Create a symbolic link to "data.txt" in the /var/tmp/ directory:
$ ln -s /home/$USER/data.txt /var/tmp/data_symlink.txt

3. To verify that the links have been correctly created, you can use the ls command with the -l option, which displays file information including the target of symbolic links:
$ ls -l /home/$USER/data_hardlink.txt /var/tmp/data_symlink.txt
This command should show that "data_hardlink.txt" is a regular file (indicating that it's a hard link) and that "data_symlink.txt" is a symbolic link to "/home/$USER/data.txt".

Question 33: User Account Management and File System Permissions

As a system administrator, you are tasked with ensuring that every new user account created on your Linux system has a file named "Note" in their home directory. This file should be automatically created upon account creation. The file should have read and write permissions for the user, but no permissions for the group and others.

Explanation

To solve this task, we can leverage the /etc/skel directory. Files and directories placed in /etc/skel will be copied into a new user's home directory when the user is created with the useradd command.

Here are the steps to accomplish this:

1. Create a file named "Note" in the /etc/skel directory. You can use the touch command to create an empty file:
$ sudo touch /etc/skel/Note

2. Set the appropriate permissions for the "Note" file. We want the user to have read and write permissions, but no permissions for the group and others. We can use the chmod command to accomplish this:
$ sudo chmod 600 /etc/skel/Note

Now, every time a new user is created, they will have a file named "Note" in their home directory with the appropriate permissions.

Explanation:

- The /etc/skel directory in Linux is used as a template for new user's home directories. When a new user is created with the useradd command, files and directories from /etc/skel are copied into the new user's home directory.
- The touch command is used to create a new empty file.
- The chmod command is used to change the permissions of a file or directory. In this case, we used chmod 600, which sets read and write permissions for the user, but no permissions for the group and others (6 corresponds to read and write permissions, and 0 corresponds to no permissions).

Question 34: User Account Management and Security

As a system administrator, you are required to manage user accounts on a Linux server. Your task is to create a new user named Sam with a User ID (UID) of 1500. However, for security reasons, Sam should not have access to any interactive shell on the system.

Explanation

To accomplish this task, you can use the useradd command, which is used to create a new user or update default new user information.

Here are the steps:

1. To create a new user named Sam with a UID of 1500 and no shell access, use the following command:
`$ sudo useradd -u 1500 -s /usr/sbin/nologin Sam`

The -u option sets the user ID, and the -s option sets the login shell. The /usr/sbin/nologin shell prevents the user from logging into the system.

2. To verify the changes, use the following command:
`$ grep Sam /etc/passwd`
This command displays the user information for Sam's account.

Explanation:

- In Linux, the useradd command is used to create a new user or update default new user information.

- The -u option is used to set the user ID, and the -s option is used to set the login shell.
- The /usr/sbin/nologin shell is a special shell assigned to the user's account to prevent the user from logging into the system. This is a common practice to enhance the security of user accounts.
- The grep command is used to check the user information in the passwd file, which contains all the local user information.

Question 35: File Permissions and Access Control Lists (ACLs)

As a system administrator, you are required to manage file permissions on a Linux server. Your task is to copy the file "/etc/fstab" to "/var/tmp". After copying, you need to configure the permissions of "/var/tmp/fstab" as follows:

a. The file "/var/tmp/fstab" should be owned by the root user and belongs to the group root. It should not be executable by anyone.

b. The user Stewart should have read and write permissions to "/var/tmp/fstab".

c. The user Kevin should not have any permissions to "/var/tmp/fstab".

Explanation

1. To copy the file "/etc/fstab" to "/var/tmp", use the following command:
$ sudo cp /etc/fstab /var/tmp/

2. To change the ownership of the file to root user and root group, use the following command:
$ sudo chown root:root /var/tmp/fstab

3. To remove the executable permissions for all users, use the following command:
$ sudo chmod a-x /var/tmp/fstab

4. To give read and write permissions to user Stewart, use the following command:
$ sudo setfacl -m u:stewart:rw /var/tmp/fstab

5. To remove all permissions for user Kevin, use the following command:

`$ sudo setfacl -m u:kevin:--- /var/tmp/fstab`

6. To verify the changes, use the following command:

`$ getfacl /var/tmp/fstab`

This command displays the Access Control List (ACL) for the file.

Explanation:

In Linux, the cp command is used to copy files and directories. The chown command is used to change file owner and group. The chmod command is used to change file mode bits. The setfacl command modifies the Access Control List (ACL) for a file or directory. In this case, it's used to set specific permissions for users Stewart and Kevin. The getfacl command displays the ACLs of a file or directory.

Question 36: Secure System Administration

In a multi-node environment, Node1 and Node2 are two Linux servers. As a system administrator, you are required to set up SSH passwordless login for the user 'Sam' on Node1 to Node2. This setup should allow 'Sam' to SSH from Node1 to Node2 without being prompted for a password.

Explanation

1. Generate SSH Key Pair on Node1: As user 'Sam', generate an SSH key pair on Node1. You can use the ssh-keygen command to do this. By default, this will create a private key (id_rsa) and a public key (id_rsa.pub) in the .ssh directory under the user's home directory.

```
sam@node1:~$ ssh-keygen
```

2. Copy Public Key to Node2: Next, you need to copy the public key to Node2. You can use the ssh-copy-id command followed by the user and host (in this case, 'Sam' and 'Node2').

```
sam@node1:~$ ssh-copy-id sam@node2
```

3. Test SSH Passwordless Login: Now, you should be able to SSH from Node1 to Node2 as 'Sam' without being prompted for a password.

```
sam@node1:~$ ssh sam@node2
```

Explanation:

The ssh-keygen command generates a pair of keys: a private key and a public key. The private key is kept secret and secure on Node1, while the public key is copied to Node2. When 'Sam' initiates an SSH session from Node1 to Node2, Node2 will use the public key to encrypt a challenge message to Node1. Node1 will use the private key to decrypt the message and send it back to Node2. If Node2 can verify the decrypted challenge message, it confirms that the client has the private key and allows the SSH session, thus achieving passwordless login.

EPILOGUE

As we reach the end of "Master LFCS 2024: Unleash Your Potential," it is my hope that this book has served you well on your journey towards becoming a Linux Foundation Certified System Administrator. The knowledge you've gained, the skills you've honed, and the challenges you've overcome have all been part of a transformative process.

The six comprehensive practice exams were designed not just to prepare you for the LFCS exam, but to instill in you a deep and lasting understanding of Linux administration. Each question answered, each problem solved, has brought you one step closer to your goal.

But remember, the end of this book is not the end of your journey. In the world of technology, learning is a lifelong pursuit. There will always be new challenges to face, new problems to solve, and new knowledge to acquire.

As you move forward, may you carry with you the lessons learned from this book. May they guide you in your future endeavors, inspire you to continue learning, and help you to realize your full potential.

Thank you for choosing "Master LFCS 2024: Unleash Your Potential." Here's to your success in the LFCS exam and beyond.

The future is yours to shape.

ABOUT THE AUTHOR

Ghada Atef

Ghada Atef is a seasoned Linux expert with a passion for open-source technologies. With a deep understanding of various Linux distributions and their applications, she has authored several comprehensive guides and practice exams to help aspiring Linux professionals.

Her works include:

1. "Unofficial Red Hat RHCSA 9 (EX200) Exam Preparation 2023: Six Complete RHCSA 9 (EX200) Practice Exams with Answers (Third Edition)" - The third edition of the comprehensive guide to the RHCSA 9 (EX200) exam, featuring six complete practice exams.
2. "Mastering Ansible: A Comprehensive Guide to Automating Configuration Management and Deployment" - A detailed exploration of Ansible, providing practical knowledge on automating configuration management and deployment.
3. "Mastering Ubuntu: A Comprehensive Guide to Linux's Favorite" - An in-depth guide to using and mastering Ubuntu, one of the most popular Linux distributions.
4. "Unofficial Red Hat Certified System Administrator RHCSA 8 & 9 (EX200) Exam Preparation 2023: Six Complete RHCSA 8 & 9 Practice Exams with Answers" - A thorough preparation

guide for the RHCSA 8 & 9 (EX200) exam, featuring six complete practice exams.

5. "RHCE EX294 Mastery: Six Practice Exams for Exam Success" - A comprehensive guide offering detailed answers to ace the Red Hat Certified Engineer EX294 Exam.

6. "Unofficial Red Hat RHCSA 9 (EX200) Exam Preparation 2023: Master the Red Hat RHCSA 9 (EX200) Exam with Confidence" - An online course designed to build confidence and knowledge for the RHCSA 9 (EX200) exam.

Ghada's work is characterized by its practical approach, clear explanations, and real-world relevance. Her dedication to helping others master Linux is evident in the depth and breadth of her work. Whether you're a beginner just starting out or a seasoned professional looking to validate your skills, Ghada's books and courses are an invaluable resource on your journey.

BOOKS BY THIS AUTHOR

Unofficial Rhcsa 8 & 9 (Ex200) Complete Reference: Rhel 8 & 9

"Unofficial RHCSA 8 & 9 (EX200) Complete Reference: RHEL 8 & 9" is a comprehensive guide that covers all the topics and objectives of the Red Hat Certified System Administrator (RHCSA) exam for RHEL 8 and 9. Whether you're a beginner or an experienced Linux user, this book provides you with the knowledge and skills to become proficient in managing and maintaining RHEL systems. From installation and configuration to system management, networking, security, and troubleshooting, this book covers everything you need to know to pass the RHCSA exam and become a certified system administrator. With clear explanations, practical examples, and real-world scenarios, "Unofficial RHCSA 8 & 9 (EX200) Complete Reference: RHEL 8 & 9" is an essential resource for anyone preparing for the RHCSA exam or seeking to improve their RHEL skills.

Mastering Ansible: A Comprehensive Guide To Automating Configuration Management And Deployment

"Mastering Ansible: A Comprehensive Guide to Automating Configuration Management and Deployment" is an in-depth guide to Ansible, a popular open-source tool for automating infrastructure as code.

The book covers everything from the basics of Ansible to advanced topics such as modules, plugins, roles, and dynamic inventory. It provides detailed guidance on how to write efficient, modular, and reusable playbooks, and how to use Ansible to automate a wide range of tasks, from provisioning servers to deploying applications.

The book also includes best practices, tips, and tricks for working effectively with Ansible, as well as use cases and real-world examples.

Whether you're a beginner or an experienced user, "Mastering Ansible" will help you become a master of Ansible and take your automation skills to the next level.

Unofficial Red Hat Certified Engineer (Rhce) Ex294 Exam Guide: A Comprehensive Study Resource For Red Hat Enterprise Linux 9

Looking to become a Red Hat Certified Engineer (RHCE)? Look no further than "Unofficial Red Hat Certified Engineer (RHCE) EX294 Exam Guide"! This comprehensive study resource is designed to help you pass the RHCE EX294 exam with ease, providing in-depth coverage of all exam objectives and six complete practice exams to help you sharpen your skills. With its clear explanations, helpful tips, and real-world scenarios, this book is an essential tool for anyone looking to succeed on the RHCE EX294 exam and take their Linux skills to the next level. So why wait? Get your copy today and start preparing for exam success!

Mastering Ubuntu: A Comprehensive Guide To Linux's Favorite Distribution

Looking to master one of the most popular Linux distributions around? Look no further than "Mastering Ubuntu"! This comprehensive guide takes you on a journey from beginner to expert, with step-by-step tutorials and practical examples to help you get the most out of your Ubuntu system. Whether you're a developer, sysadmin, or just a curious user, "Mastering Ubuntu" has everything you need to take your skills to the next level. From installation and configuration to networking, security, and beyond, this book is your ultimate resource for mastering Ubuntu.

Learn Pycharm Ide For Kids: Using Pycharm Python Ide Community Edition

Looking for a fun and engaging way to introduce your child to the world of programming? Look no further than "Learn PyCharm IDE for Kids: Using PyCharm Python IDE Community Edition." This book offers a comprehensive guide to the PyCharm Python IDE, one of the most popular tools for programming in Python. With clear and easy-to-follow instructions, your child will learn how to use PyCharm to write and run Python code, as well as how to debug and troubleshoot their programs. Whether your child is a complete beginner or has some programming experience, "Learn PyCharm IDE for Kids" is the perfect resource to help them take their coding skills to the next level.

Unofficial Red Hat Rhcsa 9 (Ex200) Exam Preparation 2023: Six Complete Rhcsa 9 (Ex200) Practice Exams With Answers (Third Edition)

Looking to ace the Red Hat RHCSA 9 (EX200) exam? Look no further than the "Unofficial Red Hat RHCSA 9 (EX200) Exam Preparation 2023" book. With six complete practice exams for RHCSA 9, this book is the ultimate study resource for anyone preparing to take the RHCSA exam. Whether you're a beginner or an experienced professional, these practice exams will test your knowledge and skills, giving you the confidence you need to pass the RHCSA exam with flying colors. With answers and detailed explanations included, you'll be able to review and strengthen your understanding of key concepts, commands, and techniques. Don't take the RHCSA exam without this essential study guide!

Rhce Ex294 Mastery: Six Practice Exams For Exam Success

This book, "RHCE EX294 Mastery: Six Practice Exams for Exam Success," is your comprehensive guide to achieving RHCE certification. It provides the tools, strategies, and in-depth knowledge to confidently ace the RHCE EX294 exam and establish yourself as a true RHEL expert.

Command Line Mastery

A Comprehensive Guide to Linux and Bash: 615 MCQs with detailed explanations on Filesystem, Process Management, Permissions, Networking, and Bash Scripting

THANK YOU!

www.ingramcontent.com/pod-product-compliance
Lightning Source LLC
LaVergne TN
LVHW051220050326
832903LV00028B/2176